SIMPLY
GLUTEN-FREE
& DAIRY-FREE

2 (

SIMPLY
GLUTEN-FREE
& DAIRY-FREE

BREAKFASTS • LUNCHES • TREATS • DINNERS • DESSERTS

GRACE CHEETHAM

dbp

DUNCAN BAIRD PUBLISHERS

LONDON

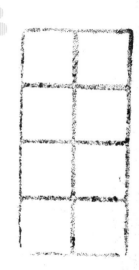

SIMPLY GLUTEN-FREE & DAIRY-FREE
Grace Cheetham

First published in the United Kingdom and Ireland
in 2011 by Duncan Baird Publishers, an imprint of
Watkins Publishing Limited
Sixth Floor
75 Wells Street
London W1T 3QH

A member of Osprey Group

This paperback edition first published in 2013

Editor: Nicole Bator
Managing Designer: Suzanne Tuhrim
Commissioned photography: William Lingwood,
except for the following by Toby Scott p.5 (bottom right),
59, 105, 141
Photographer's Assistant: Isobel Wield
Food Stylist: Bridget Sargeson
Food Stylist's Assistants: Emily Jonzen and Jack Sargeson
Prop Stylist: Rachel Jukes

A CIP record for this book is available from the
British Library

In loving memory of Pa, who was
the most wonderful father.

10 9 8 7 6 5 4 3 2 1

ISBN: 978-1-84899-092-0

Typeset in Cambria
Colour reproduction by Bright Arts, Malaysia
Printed in China

Notes on the recipes
Unless otherwise stated:
Use medium fruit and vegetables
Use fresh ingredients, including herbs and spices
Do not mix metric and imperial measurements
1 tsp = 5ml 1 tbsp = 15ml 1 cup = 250ml

Author's acknowledgments
Huge thanks to everyone who has worked to produce such
a beautiful book, especially my brilliant editor, Nicole; my
Americanizer, Beverly; Suzanne for her design; William for
his photography; and Bridget for her food styling. Many
thanks, also, to Uzma for my author photo and to Duncan,
Bob and Roger, and the Sales teams. I couldn't have written
this book without the patience and support of my gorgeous
husband and daughter, Peter and Zoë, who light up my life –
and who put up with me writing and testing late at night
and at the weekends, and tasted everything for me.

Coeliac UK licence number CUK-M-141

Symbols

 GLUTEN-FREE
Contains no gluten-based grains or grain products, including wheat, barley, rye, oats, spelt, kamut, triticale, wheat bran, oat bran and barley malt syrup.

 DAIRY-FREE
Contains no milk, cheese, cream, yogurt, butter or other dairy products from cows, goats or sheep.

 YEAST-FREE
Contains no ingredients with added yeast, including sourdough and yeast breads, all vinegars, wine, beer and other alcoholic beverages, yeast extract, Marmite, tamari soy sauce and miso.

 SOYA-FREE
Contains no soya products, including soya beans, soya milk, soya yogurt, soya cream, soya cheese, tofu, tempeh, soy sauce and soya-based margarines.

 EGG-FREE
Contains no eggs or egg products.

 NUT-FREE
Contains no nuts (almonds, Brazil nuts, cashew nuts, chestnuts, coconut, hazelnuts, macadamia nuts, peanuts, pecans, pine nuts, pistachio nuts and walnuts) or nut oils.

 SEED-FREE
Contains no seeds (hemp seeds, linseeds, pumpkin seeds, sesame seeds and sunflower seeds) or seed oils, including vegetable oil and seed-based margarines.

 CITRUS-FREE
Contains no citrus fruit or zest, including oranges, grapefruit, lemons, limes, clementines, satsumas and tangerines.

 VEGETARIAN
Contains no meat, poultry, game, fish, shellfish or animal by-products. May include eggs or honey.

Contents

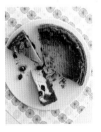

Introduction

For many people, food is a wonderful, enriching part of their life. But for those who have coeliac disease or have allergies or intolerances, it can seem like a nightmare. When I was first diagnosed with intolerances, it felt as if the foods I was reacting to had become poisons to me, and that the whole culinary world had become a hostile place. It took time to learn to adapt my diet, but once I learnt to make meals that I didn't react to, my relationship with food evolved. I accepted the changes and started to love food again.

I discovered ingredients that worked as alternatives to gluten and dairy, as well as ones that are naturally gluten-free and dairy-free. I worked out how to use different flours, grains, milks, cheeses and yogurts, and found new ways to add flavour and taste.

As my life became busier, I learnt how to fit my diet into my daily routine, making food that I could easily take with me to work, when I was travelling or before an evening out. Then when my daughter, Zoë, was born, I had to find ways to make recipes as quickly and simply as possible.

I've written this book in the hope that the recipes will inspire you to love food again, too. I've included dishes from all over the world, many of which use alternative ingredients to create gluten- and dairy-free versions of classics. There are recipes for all aspects of your daily life, including breakfasts you can eat on-the-run, lunches you can pack up and take with you, dinners you can cook for friends and family, and mouth-watering treats for any time of the day. But more importantly, I've based the book around simplicity. You'll find recipes that really are stress-free, with ingredients that work brilliantly and techniques that would make a purist cook wince! Whip up the Brioche with Caramelized Peaches or Salmon en Croûte, for example, using a food processor to do all the work for you, and you don't have to spend time kneading the dough or the pastry. Whizz cashew nuts in a blender to make cream for Chicken Tikka Masala or a Strawberry Pannacotta. Or use an electric mixer to make the crust for Herb- and Olive-Crusted Lamb or the mixture for a Chocolate Birthday Cake.

For me, cooking is like alchemy – you take some ingredients and make a dish that can nurture you physically and emotionally. You can heap nutrients into your body – boosting your immune system, energy levels and vitality, and helping your body to alleviate symptoms and start to heal itself. Then you can just sit back and enjoy the gorgeous tastes, textures and aromas of the recipes you've created with each delicious bite.

Salt and Pepper Squid, page 64 >

GETTING STARTED

It's well worth stocking up on lots of different ingredients so that you have them to hand when you want to make something. Fill your cupboards with gluten-free pastas, noodles, polenta and different types of rice. You can get fusilli, penne, spaghetti and lasagne sheets made from corn and rice very easily. You'll also find wonderful varieties of rice noodles – thick and thin – as well as noodles made purely from buckwheat and glass noodles made from mung beans. Stock up, too, on dairy-free alternatives, such as margarine made from vegetable oils or soya, soya yogurts, soya cream cheese and soya cheeses. They're fantastically useful, and most of them last for a considerable amount of time in your fridge.

For most of the baking recipes, I've used a mixture of rice, gram (also known as chickpea flour or besan) and maize flours because they're easily available and they combine brilliantly in terms of flavour and consistency. I've also added potato flour to the breads to ensure that they don't taste dry, like some gluten-free versions do. I've shown you how you can use other flours, too, so that you can discover how to work with the different tastes and textures – and also benefit nutritionally. In the Buckwheat and Blueberry Pancakes, for example, I've used the nutty-tasting buckwheat flour, but combined it with sweet blueberries and honey so that the flavours sing. In the Chocolate Birthday Cake, I've added chestnut flour, which, unlike most gluten-free flours, has great binding properties – but its distinctive taste can sometimes overpower other flavours. In this recipe, though, it goes perfectly with the rich, sweet chocolate and sharply sweet raspberries. And when I've used quinoa flour in the richly-sweet Fruit Cake, I've masked its strong taste with different dried fruits and ground almonds.

Quinoa is a wonderfully nutritious ingredient. I've used the flakes in the full-on fruity, nutty Apricot, Cranberry and Goji Berry Granola (as opposed to buckwheat flakes in the Muesli) and the whole grain itself in the Roasted Vegetables and Quinoa, which shows how it works best with strong, bold flavours.

Amaranth is another wonderfood to add to your storecupboard. The grain dates back to the time of the Aztecs and the Incas and can be used as an alternative to couscous, such as in the Pomegranate Amaranth. It's also a lovely bulking agent in the mixture for the Herb- and Olive-Crusted Lamb, giving the crust a really crunchy texture.

Cashew nuts make brilliant milk and cream. The textures are smooth and creamy and the nutty taste very subtle, making it hugely versatile. You'll find it in the dairy-free version of the fiery Chicken Tikka Masala, as well as in Strawberry Pannacotta and in the icing used in the Chocolate Birthday Cake.

Almonds are a classic gluten-free ingredient, used in many different cuisines around the world. Ground into a flour, they give sweet moistness in baking, as well as a lovely light texture, such as in the Almond Cake. But they can also serve as a wonderful dairy-free alternative. As with cashew nuts, you can whizz almonds into a deliciously creamy milk or cream in your food processor or blender and make, for example, the irresistible almond cream to spread over the Almond Cake.

Coconut milk has finally lost its bad reputation and can stand tall as a dairy-free alternative. While it does contain saturated fats, it's now acknowledged that they are different to the ones in meat and, instead of being stored as fat in our bodies, they can provide a fantastic source of immune-boosting energy. Add in the high levels of vitamins that coconut milk contains, and you can tuck into the Chicken and Coconut Soup, for example, or the Prawn and Butternut Squash Curry without any guilt.

It's also worth making sure you always have gluten-free tamari soy sauce in your cupboard, as well as a good gluten- and dairy-free stock powder, gluten-free baking powder and lower-GI sweeteners, such as fruit sugar, xylitol or agave syrup. Pick up a pot of xanthan gum, too – now widely available. It's great at holding gluten-free baked goods together. Also stock up on cornflour for thickening soups, stews, sauces and fillings, and for creating a crispy coating, such as with the Salt and Pepper Squid.

As an alternative to cornflour, I've also used kuzu, which is made from the root of a Japanese plant. Added to the Slow-Cooked Beef, for example, it creates a thick sauce. I've also used agar agar flakes instead of gelatine. Naturally processed from sea vegetables, these flakes are a staple in many Asian cuisines.

Sea vegetables themselves are brilliant. They add an exotic dimension to any dish, such as in the Arame and Cashew Nut Stir-fry, and they supercharge the nutrient count of the dish. Add kombu to the Buckwheat Soba Noodles with Tofu, for example, and you create a fantastically nutritious stock.

I've used a couple of other unusual ingredients – umeboshi paste in the Duck with Plums and pomegranate molasses in the Cannellini Dip, the Lamb Burgers and the Fig and Date Fruit Bars. Again, these are nutritious products that add delicious, distinctive depth of flavour to the recipes in which they're used.

As well as super healthy recipes, I've also put in lots of treats. You may want to keep sweet recipes to a minimum if you're watching your sugar consumption, but even if you only indulge every now and then, I wanted to make sure there would be masses of choice. Choose from breakfasts that will tempt you out of bed in the morning; biscuits, cakes and tarts to fill your day with delight; and desserts for true indulgence. Most of them contain significantly less sugar than conventional recipes and a lot have additional nutrients added. For example, the figs in the Chocolate and Fig Cookies add high levels of calcium, potassium and fibre. And the apples piled over the Apple Cake are rich in both soluble and insoluble fibre, which ease digestive complaints and help to detox your body.

In terms of equipment, try switching to PTFE-free non-stick pans that don't release toxins, especially when frying at a high temperature. A food processor and blender, as well as a mini food processor or spice mill, are essential. Use them to spend minimal time and effort making the recipes – and to cheat whenever possible! I find it helps to keep this equipment on my kitchen worktops. Without stopping to think, I can quickly chop tiny foods, like chillies, not to mention more time-consuming or tough things, such as nuts or lemongrass. And, oh, the complete and utter joy of mixing dough and pastry in a food processor!

Baking with gluten-free flours can get messy! I get the best results when the dough has more liquid in it than a traditional dough, but this does mean the dough is very sticky. Gluten-free pastry can burn easily, too, so I cover it with greaseproof paper or baking parchment. But don't worry – I've put step-by-step instructions in the recipes, showing you how to handle the various doughs.

HELPING YOUR BODY TO HEAL

If you have coeliac disease and have to avoid gluten, or suffer from other problems such as eczema, asthma, migraines, nausea, vomiting, bloating, bowel problems, irritable bowel syndrome (IBS), chronic fatigue syndrome (CFS or ME) or depression, you may find that certain foods aggravate your condition and that avoiding these foods will help enormously – that your symptoms will clear and you'll begin to feel much, much better. But your body's long-term reactions might well have had a hugely debilitating effect. Your adrenaline levels may have been high, for example, causing your immune system

to struggle, and you may not have been digesting food properly or assimilating the nutrients. So it is vital to replenish your body's store of vitamins, minerals, phytochemicals and other nutrients so that your body can start to heal itself.

Try to buy organic produce whenever you can, especially meat, fish and eggs, and to eat pure, natural foods. Avoid additives or preservatives and check food labels to see what's in the foods you buy – look for nitrate-free hams, for example, and unsulphured dried apricots.

Eat stacks of fresh fruit and vegetables, preferably local, seasonal versions that will have higher nutrient levels, as well as far superior flavour. Fill up with protein- and fibre-rich beans and pulses, including Puy lentils, chickpeas, butter beans and cannellini beans. Add whole or ground nuts and seeds to your meals throughout the day, especially to juices and smoothies, muesli mixtures, salads, stir-frys, biscuits, cakes and desserts. Go for stable oils, such as olive, rapeseed (canola) or safflower, and add in essential fatty acids, particularly omega-3, through ingredients such as oily fish like salmon, sardines and tuna, walnuts, hemp seeds and linseeds. Drink herbal teas and pure, life-giving water as often as you can.

ONWARDS AND UPWARDS

Above all, the recipes in this book are to be enjoyed. Dive into them with your family and friends and discover ingredients and dishes that you love – whether for a quick snack, a super-healthy meal or a truly magical feast.

Summer Pudding, page 159 >

Basic Recipes

White Sauce

Makes **about 650ml/22fl oz/2⅔ cups**   Preparation time **5 minutes**   Cooking time **20 minutes**

40g/1½oz dairy-free margarine

30g/1oz/scant ¼ cup rice flour

1½ tbsp gram flour

1½ tbsp maize flour

550–700ml/19–24fl oz/2¼–2¾ cups Vegetable
   Stock (see page 21) or vegetable stock made
   with gluten- and dairy-free stock powder

sea salt and freshly ground black pepper

1   Melt the dairy-free margarine in a heavy-based saucepan over a low heat. Stir in the flours, then remove the pan from the heat and gradually add 375ml/13fl oz/1½ cups of the stock, stirring continuously. Return the pan to a medium heat and bring to the boil, stirring continuously as it thickens. Gradually add another 175ml/6fl oz/¾ cup of the remaining stock. If the sauce gets lumpy, beat with a whisk until smooth.

2   Turn the heat down to low and simmer very gently for 10 minutes, stirring frequently to prevent the sauce from sticking to the pan. Gradually stir in the remaining stock, if necessary, to make a smooth sauce that is thick, but still runny. Season lightly with salt and pepper.

Roasted Tomato and Pepper Sauce

Makes **about 1.25l/44fl oz/5 cups**   Preparation time **5 minutes**   Cooking time **30 minutes**

3 red, orange or yellow peppers, quartered
   and deseeded

10 tomatoes, halved

1 large onion, peeled and quartered

3 tbsp olive oil

2 garlic cloves

sea salt and freshly ground black pepper

1   Preheat the oven to 180°C/350°F/gas 4. Put the peppers, tomatoes and onion on two baking sheets and drizzle with the oil. Bake for 10 minutes, then add the garlic and bake for another 20 minutes until soft and starting to brown.

2   Transfer to a blender and blend until smooth. Season lightly with salt and pepper.

Custard

Makes **about 500ml/17fl oz/2 cups**   Preparation time **5 minutes**   Cooking time **20 minutes**

500ml/17fl oz/2 cups soya milk

1 tbsp cornflour

5 large egg yolks

100g/3½oz/scant ½ cup fruit sugar

or caster sugar

1 tsp vanilla extract

1   Heat the soya milk in a heavy-based saucepan over a low heat until almost boiling. While the soya milk is warming, mix the cornflour and 1 tablespoon water together in a large mixing bowl to form a smooth paste. Add the egg yolks and sugar and whisk until the mixture thickens. Gradually add the hot milk and stir until well mixed.

2   Pour the mixture into a clean saucepan, add the vanilla extract and cook over a low heat, stirring frequently, for 10–15 minutes until it forms a thick custard. Be careful not to overheat or the custard may curdle; if it does, beat with a whisk until smooth.

Cashew Nut Cream

Makes **about 650ml/22fl oz/2⅔ cups**   Preparation time **10 minutes, plus at least 12 hours soaking**

300g/10½oz/scant 2 cups cashew nuts

1   Put the nuts in a bowl, cover with cold water and leave to soak at room temperature overnight or for at least 12 hours.

2   Drain and rinse the nuts thoroughly, then put them in a blender. Add 250ml/9fl oz/ 1 cup water and blend for 10 minutes or until smooth.

White Bread

Makes **1 loaf (about 16 slices)**   Preparation time **15 minutes, plus 30 minutes rising**
Cooking time **50 minutes**

120g/4¼oz/⅔ cup potato flour

50g/1¾oz/scant ½ cup gram flour

50g/1¾oz/⅓ cup maize flour

150g/5½oz/heaped ¾ cup brown rice flour

1 tsp sea salt, crushed

1 tsp fruit sugar or caster sugar

1 tsp gluten-free baking powder

1 tsp xanthan gum

1 tbsp dried active yeast

2 tbsp olive oil

dairy-free margarine, for greasing

1 Sift the flours, salt, sugar, gluten-free baking powder, xanthan gum and yeast into a large mixing bowl and, using a metal whisk, whisk to mix together. Add the oil and whisk again, then add 400ml/14fl oz/scant 1⅔ cups warm water and whisk for about 1 minute to aerate the dough. It will be sticky. Alternatively, sift the flours, salt, sugar, gluten-free baking powder, xanthan gum and yeast into the bowl of a food processor with the dough blade attached and blend to mix together. Add the oil and blend again, then add 400ml/14fl oz/scant 1⅔ cups warm water and process for about 5 minutes to aerate the dough.

2 Transfer the dough to a bowl, cover with cling film and leave to rise for 30 minutes.

3 Preheat the oven to 200°C/400°F/gas 6 and lightly grease a 900g/2lb loaf tin with dairy-free margarine. Spoon the dough into the tin and smooth the surface with the back of a metal spoon.

4 Bake for 45–50 minutes until the bread is golden brown. Turn out of the tin and tap the bottom. If it sounds hollow, it is done. If not, return the bread to the tin and bake for another 5 minutes, then test again to see whether it is done. Transfer to a wire rack to cool.

basic recipes

Rosemary Focaccia

Makes **1 loaf (about 10 pieces)**   Preparation time **15 minutes, plus 30 minutes rising**
Cooking time **50 minutes**

120g/4¼oz/⅔ cup potato flour

50g/1¾oz/scant ½ cup gram flour

50g/1¾oz/⅓ cup maize flour

150g/5½oz/heaped ¾ cup brown rice flour

1 tsp sea salt, crushed, plus extra for sprinkling

1 tsp xanthan gum

1 tbsp dried active yeast

4 tbsp olive oil, plus extra for greasing

1 handful of rosemary leaves, chopped

1   Sift the flours, salt, xanthan gum and yeast into a large mixing bowl and, using a metal whisk, whisk to mix together. Add 3 tablespoons of the oil and whisk again, then add 400ml/ 14fl oz/scant 1⅔ cups warm water and whisk for about 1 minute to aerate the dough. It will be sticky. Alternatively, sift the flours, salt, xanthan gum and yeast into the bowl of a food processor with the dough blade attached and blend to mix together. Add 3 tablespoons of the oil and blend again. Add 400ml/14fl oz/scant 1⅔ cups warm water and process for about 5 minutes to aerate the dough.

2   Transfer the dough to a bowl, cover with cling film and leave to rise for 30 minutes.

3   Preheat the oven to 200°C/400°F/gas 6 and lightly grease a 20cm/8in cake tin with a little oil. Spoon the dough into the tin and smooth the surface with the back of a metal spoon. Drizzle the remaining oil over the top, then sprinkle with the rosemary and salt.

4   Bake for 45–50 minutes until the bread is golden brown. Turn out of the tin and tap the bottom. If it sounds hollow, it is done. If not, return the bread to the tin and bake for another 5 minutes, then test again to see whether it is done. Transfer to a wire rack to cool.

basic recipes

Flatbread

Makes **8**   Preparation time **25 minutes, plus 1 hour rising**   Cooking time **25 minutes**

2 tsp dried active yeast

200g/7oz/heaped 1 cup brown rice flour

150g/5½oz/heaped 1⅓ cups gram flour

150g/5½oz/heaped ¾ cup potato flour

1 tsp sea salt, crushed

1½ tbsp xanthan gum

2 tbsp olive oil, plus extra for greasing

1   In a small mixing bowl, whisk together the yeast and 400ml/14fl oz/scant 1⅔ cups warm water and leave to stand for 10 minutes.

2   Sift the flours, salt and xanthan gum into a large mixing bowl and, using a metal whisk, whisk to mix together. Add the oil and whisk again, then add the yeast mixture and whisk for about 1 minute to aerate the dough. It will be sticky. Alternatively, sift the flours, salt and xanthan gum into the bowl of a food processor with the dough blade attached and blend to mix together. Add the oil and blend again, then add the yeast mixture and process for about 5 minutes to aerate the dough.

3   Transfer the dough to a bowl, cover with cling film and leave to rise for 1 hour.

4   Preheat the oven to 200°C/400°F/gas 6. Divide the dough into 8 equal portions and put 2 portions on a piece of baking parchment, leaving enough room to shape each one into a flatbread. Grease another piece of baking parchment and put it, oiled-side down, over the dough. Using your hands, flatten and shape both pieces of dough into flatbreads, each about 5mm/¼in thick. Remove the top layer of baking parchment. Transfer the flatbreads and bottom sheet of baking parchment to a baking sheet. Repeat with the remaining pieces of dough and arrange them on three additional baking sheets. Bake for 20–25 minutes until lightly golden.

Corn Tortillas

Makes **8**   Preparation time **10 minutes, plus 15 minutes resting**   Cooking time **10 minutes**

250g/9oz/2¼ cups masa harina   **1 tsp sea salt, crushed**

1   Sift the masa harina and salt into the bowl of a food processor with the dough blade attached. Add 325ml/11fl oz/scant 1⅓ cups warm water and process for about 5 minutes to aerate the dough.

2   Transfer the dough to a mixing bowl, cover with cling film and leave to rest for 15 minutes.

3   Divide the dough into 8 equal portions and shape them into balls. On a work surface, put 1 of the balls between two pieces of baking parchment and, using a rolling pin, roll it out into a thin circle, about 20cm/8in in diameter and 1mm/1⁄32in thick.

4   Heat a frying pan or griddle pan over a medium-high heat until hot. Cook the tortilla for about 30 seconds until it has brown spots underneath, then turn it over and cook for a few more seconds until it puffs up. Using a spatula, transfer the tortilla to a clean, slightly dampened tea towel and wrap it up to keep it warm and soft. Repeat with the remaining pieces of dough.

basic recipes

Light Pastry

Makes **enough for 1 x 20cm/8in tart tin or 4 x 10cm/4in tartlet tins**   Preparation time **15 minutes,** plus 30 minutes chilling   Cooking time **15 minutes**

1 potato, peeled and cut into large chunks

100g/3½oz/heaped ½ cup brown rice flour, plus
    extra as needed

40g/1½oz/heaped ⅓ cup gram flour

40g/1½oz/scant ⅓ cup maize flour

½ tsp sea salt, crushed, plus extra to season

1 tsp xanthan gum

125g/4½oz chilled dairy-free margarine, diced,
    plus extra for greasing

1 large egg, beaten

1   Put the potato in a saucepan and cover with cold water. Bring to the boil over a high heat, then turn the heat down to medium and simmer, covered, for 15 minutes or until tender. Drain, then mash until smooth.

2   Sift the flours, salt and xanthan gum into the bowl of a food processor. Add the dairy-free margarine and blend until the mixture resembles fine breadcrumbs, then add the mashed potato and blend for a few seconds until mixed in. Add the egg and blend for 20–30 seconds until the mixture comes away from the sides of the bowl and forms a sticky dough. There should be a little extra moisture at the base of the bowl. If it is too dry, gradually blend in 1–2 tablespoons chilled water. If it is too sticky, add a little rice flour.

3   Shape the pastry into a ball, wrap it in cling film and chill in the fridge for 30 minutes.

Breakfasts

Breakfast in our home is either hectic and rushed or leisurely, depending on whether it's a weekday or the weekend. Whether you're running out the door or able to sit back and relax, here are recipes that will work brilliantly – and they're all delicious. Boost your energy levels for the day with Pineapple, Strawberry, and Passionfruit Smoothie, for example; or pack up some Brioche with Caramelized Peaches or Mango and Macadamia Muffins to take with you. Make pancake batter or bread the night before and tuck into Sweetcorn Pancakes or French Toast with Pears the next morning. Or cook up Spanish-Style Eggs and invite friends and family round to share them with you.

Apricot, Cranberry and Goji Berry Granola, page 37 >

Smoothies make a wonderful start to the day. Full of vitamins, minerals and protein, they give you energy and vitality.

Mango and Pomegranate Smoothie

Serves **4**   Preparation time **10 minutes**

2 large mangoes

250ml/9fl oz/1 cup pomegranate juice

250ml/9fl oz/1 cup unflavoured soya yogurt

1 tbsp linseeds

1   Using a sharp knife, carefully slice the mango down both sides, avoiding the stone. On the inside of each slice, cut the flesh into squares, cutting down to the peel but not piercing it, and scoop out with a spoon. Peel the remains of the mango and slice the flesh from the stone. Put all of the mango flesh in a blender or food processor.

2   Add all of the remaining ingredients and blend until smooth and creamy. Serve immediately.

Pineapple, Strawberry and Passionfruit Smoothie

Serves **4**   Preparation time **10 minutes**

1 pineapple

400g/14oz/2⅔ cups strawberries, hulled

4 passionfruits, halved and seeds scooped out

400ml/14fl oz/scant 1⅔ cups coconut milk

2 tbsp agave syrup

1   Trim the woody base and green top off the pineapple and, holding it upright, slice off and discard the skin, including the 'eyes'. Slice the flesh down the length of the fruit all around into long, thin slices, cutting around the core, then chop the flesh.

2   Put the pineapple and all of the remaining ingredients in a blender or food processor and blend until smooth and creamy. Serve immediately.

I adore juices! These recipes give you maximum nutrition along with either fruity, minty flavours or the taste of zingy ginger with sweet vegetables.

Apple, Blueberry and Grape Juice

Serves **2**   Preparation time **5 minutes**

½ lime, halved

150g/5½oz/1 cup blueberries

2 large apples, quartered and stems removed

500g/1lb 2oz seedless grapes, stems removed

1 small handful of mint leaves

1   Scoop the flesh of the lime from the peel with a spoon and put it through an electric juicer. Juice all of the remaining ingredients and serve immediately.

Carrot, Pepper, Tomato and Kiwi Juice

Serves **2**   Preparation time **5 minutes**

6 carrots, scrubbed, topped and tailed

1 red pepper, quartered

4 tomatoes, quartered

4 kiwi fruits, peeled and quartered

2.5cm/1in piece peeled root ginger

1   Put all of the ingredients through an electric juicer and serve immediately.

Here I'm using two of Australia's food heroes – macadamia nuts and mango. The first time I went to Sydney, some friends gave us boxes of gorgeously sweet mangoes and fresh macadamias. Great memories!

Mango and Macadamia Muffins

Makes **10**   Preparation time **15 minutes**   Cooking time **30 minutes**

1 large, very ripe mango

75g/2½oz dairy-free margarine, softened

75g/2½oz/scant ½ cup fruit sugar or
     caster sugar

2 large eggs

80ml/2½fl oz/⅓ cup unflavoured soya yogurt

100g/3½oz/heaped ½ cup brown rice flour

50g/1¾oz/scant ½ cup gram flour

50g/1¾oz/⅓ cup maize flour

2 tsp gluten-free baking powder

½ tsp xanthan gum

50g/1¾oz dried mango, cut into small pieces

100g/3½oz/⅔ cup macadamia nuts, finely
     chopped

1   Preheat the oven to 180°C/350°F/gas 4 and put 10 paper muffin cases in a muffin tin. Using a sharp knife, carefully slice the mango down both sides, avoiding the stone. On the inside of each slice, cut the flesh into very small squares, cutting down to the peel but not piercing it, then scoop it out with a spoon. Peel the remaining parts of the mangoes and cut the flesh off the stones and cut into very small pieces. Set aside.

2   Put the dairy-free margarine and sugar in a large mixing bowl and, using an electric mixer, beat well until light and fluffy. Gradually beat in the eggs, one at a time, then beat in the soya yogurt.

3   Sift in the flours, gluten-free baking powder and xanthan gum and stir quickly until mixed. Be careful not to overmix, and don't worry if there are some lumps in the mixture. Stir in the fresh mango pieces, dried mango and nuts, then spoon the mixture into the muffin cases, filling each one about two-thirds full.

4   Bake for 25–30 minutes until well risen, golden brown and just firm to the touch or until a skewer inserted into the centre comes out clean. Remove from the oven and eat the muffins warm or transfer them in their paper cases to a wire rack to cool.

My favourite combination of gluten-free flours is rice, gram and maize because they balance each other in terms of taste and texture. In this recipe, I've used potato flour as well, to add moistness.

Brioche with Caramelized Peaches

Serves 4   Preparation time **20 minutes, plus 4 hours rising**   Cooking time **30 minutes**

100g/3½oz/heaped ½ cup potato flour

50g/1¾oz/scant ½ cup gram flour

50g/1¾oz/⅓ cup maize flour

150g/5½oz/heaped ¾ cup brown rice flour

1 tsp sea salt, crushed

1 tsp xanthan gum

2 tsp dried active yeast

165g/5¾oz dairy-free margarine, chilled and
cut into small pieces, plus extra for greasing

100ml/3½fl oz/scant ½ cup soya milk

4 eggs

6 tbsp fruit sugar or caster sugar

4 peaches, pitted and sliced into 8 pieces

1   Sift the flours, salt, xanthan gum and yeast into the bowl of a food processor with the dough blade attached and blend until mixed together. Add 150g/5½oz of the dairy-free margarine and blend until the mixture resembles breadcrumbs. Add the soya milk, 3 of the eggs and 3 tablespoons of the sugar and process for about 5 minutes to aerate the dough. Put the dough in a large bowl, cover with cling film and leave to rise for 1 hour.

2   Grease a 12-hole muffin tin with dairy-free margarine. Stir the brioche dough thoroughly and pour evenly into the muffin tin. Cover loosely with cling film and leave to prove for 3 hours until light, puffy and doubled in size.

3   Preheat the oven to 200°C/400°F/gas 6. Beat the remaining egg and brush it over the brioches, using a pastry brush. Bake for 20 minutes until golden brown. Leave to cool for 2–3 minutes, then turn out of the tin and transfer to a wire rack before serving.

4   While the brioche are cooling, put the remaining margarine and sugar in a saucepan and heat over a low heat until the dairy-free margarine has melted and the sugar has dissolved. Bring to the boil over a high heat, then turn the heat down again to low and simmer for 4–5 minutes until the mixture has caramelized slightly and become syrupy. Add the peaches to the saucepan and shake the pan to cover the peaches in the syrup. Cook for 2–3 minutes until tender, continuing to shake the pan occasionally. Serve immediately with the brioche.

Frozen sweetcorn is a wonderful staple ingredient. Sweet-flavoured and filling, it works brilliantly in these pancakes.

Sweetcorn Pancakes

Makes **12 pancakes**   Preparation time **10 minutes**   Cooking time **30 minutes**

8 tomatoes

350g/12oz/2⅓ cups sweetcorn

50g/1¾oz/heaped ¼ cup brown rice flour

50g/1¾oz/⅓ cup maize flour

a pinch of salt

1 tsp gluten-free baking powder

2 large eggs

250ml/9fl oz/1 cup soya cream

1 tbsp olive oil

freshly ground black pepper

2 avocados, peeled, pitted and sliced, to serve

1 large handful of rocket leaves, to serve

1   Preheat the grill to high. Grill the tomatoes for 3–4 minutes until just starting to turn brown, then set aside.

2   Put the sweetcorn in a steamer and steam over a high heat for 3–4 minutes until just tender.

3   Sift the flours, salt and gluten-free baking powder into a large mixing bowl. Beat together the eggs and soya cream in another bowl. Make a well in the centre of the flour mixture and add the egg mixture. Beat slowly with a wooden spoon to draw in the flours to make a smooth batter. Stir in the sweetcorn.

4   Heat the oil in a large heavy-based frying pan over a medium heat until hot. Pour 2 tablespoons of the batter into one half of the pan to make a pancake and then pour 2 more tablespoons into the other half. Cook for 2–3 minutes on each side or until golden.

5   Repeat with the remaining batter, adding more oil to the pan as needed. Stack the freshly cooked pancakes between sheets of non-stick baking parchment to prevent them from sticking together and to keep them warm. Note that the later pancakes will take less time on each side as the pan will have heated up. Season with black pepper, then serve hot with the grilled tomatoes, avocados and rocket leaves.

breakfasts

My daughter, Zoë, loves to be involved when I'm cooking. This is a great recipe to make with her because I can cook it with one hand while balancing her on my hip with the other.

French Toast with Pears

Serves **4**   Preparation time **5 minutes, plus making the bread**   Cooking time **30 minutes**

2 eggs

80ml/2½fl oz/⅓ cup soya milk

75g/2½oz/scant ½ cup fruit sugar or caster sugar

45g/1½oz dairy-free margarine

4 pears, peeled, cored and sliced lengthways

8 slices of White Bread (see page 14)

1   Put the eggs, soya milk and a scant 2 tablespoons of the sugar a large bowl. Beat well.

2   Put the remaining sugar and 30g/1oz of the dairy-free margarine in a saucepan and heat over a low heat until the margarine has melted and the sugar has dissolved. Bring to the boil over a high heat, then turn the heat down again to low and leave to simmer for 4–5 minutes until the mixture has caramelized slightly and become syrupy.

3   Add the pears and shake the pan to cover them in the syrup. Cook for 2–3 minutes until soft, continuing to shake the pan occasionally, then set aside.

4   Soak the bread in the egg mixture for 2 minutes until completely soaked. Preheat the oven to 70°C/150°F/gas ¼. Put the remaining margarine in a frying pan and heat over a medium heat until it has melted. Drain a couple of slices of the bread and fry for 2–3 minutes on each side until golden brown. Remove from the pan and keep warm in the oven while you repeat with the remaining bread. Serve hot with the pears spooned over the French toast.

breakfasts

Blueberries are the king of antioxidants, so these pancakes are a great way to start the day. To make the pancakes more substantial, I've made a thick batter with buckwheat flour, soya cream and whisked egg whites.

Buckwheat and Blueberry Pancakes

Makes **8**   Preparation time **10 minutes, plus at least 10 minutes resting**
Cooking time **20 minutes**

3 large eggs, separated

50g/1¾oz/heaped ⅓ cup buckwheat flour

50g/1¾oz/heaped ¼ cup brown rice flour

1 tsp gluten-free baking powder

a pinch of salt

250ml/9fl oz/1 cup soya cream

2 tbsp unsweetened soya milk

30–40g/1–1½oz dairy-free margarine

200g/7oz/1⅓ cups blueberries

clear honey, to serve

1   Beat the egg yolks in a large mixing bowl, then sift in the flours, gluten-free baking powder and salt and stir together. Slowly beat in the soya cream and soya milk, gradually drawing in the flours to make a thick, smooth batter.

2   Put the egg whites in a clean bowl and whisk until they form stiff peaks. With a large metal spoon, carefully fold the whisked egg whites into the batter until they are thoroughly mixed in. Cover and leave to stand for at least 10 minutes at room temperature or up to 30 minutes in the fridge.

3   Meanwhile, heat a large non-stick frying pan over a medium heat until hot. Add a little of the dairy-free margarine and heat until melted, making sure it covers the base of the pan. Pour about 7 tablespoons of the batter into the pan to form a circle. Sprinkle a small handful of the blueberries over the top and cook for 2–3 minutes or until the base of the pancake is golden. Using a large spatula, flip it over and cook for another 1–2 minutes until golden.

4   Repeat with the remaining batter to make 8 pancakes, melting more margarine in the pan as needed. Stack the pancakes between sheets of baking parchment to prevent them from sticking together and to keep them warm. Drizzle with honey and serve hot.

breakfasts

Baking the quinoa and rice flakes until golden makes them deliciously crunchy for this chewy, nutty cereal.

Apricot, Cranberry and Goji Berry Granola

Makes **8–10 servings**   Preparation time **15 minutes**   Cooking time **20 minutes**

50g/1¾oz dairy-free margarine, plus extra for greasing

80ml/2½fl oz/⅓ cup date syrup

1 tsp vanilla extract

150g/5½oz/heaped 1 cup quinoa flakes

150g/5½oz/heaped 1 cup rice flakes

50g/1¾oz/heaped ¼ cup pumpkin seeds

50g/1¾oz/scant ⅓ cup linseeds

100g/3½oz/⅔ cup almonds, chopped

100g/3½oz/⅔ cup brazil nuts, chopped

50g/1¾oz/heaped ⅓ cup hazelnuts, chopped

25g/1oz/scant ¼ cup dried goji berries

50g/1¾oz/⅓ cup dried cranberries

75g/2½oz/heaped ⅓ cup unsulphured dried apricots, chopped

100g/3½oz/2 cups coconut flakes

1   Preheat the oven to 150°C/300°F/gas 2 and grease two baking sheets with dairy-free margarine. Put the dairy-free margarine, date syrup and vanilla extract in a saucepan and heat over a low heat until the margarine has melted, stirring to make sure it is mixed well.

2   Put the quinoa flakes, rice flakes, seeds and nuts in a large bowl and mix well. Add the melted margarine mixture and stir well.

3   Divide the mixture between the two baking sheets and bake for 10 minutes until the quinoa and rice flakes are starting to turn golden. Mix in the berries, apricots and coconut and bake for another 10 minutes.

4   Stir and leave to cool completely on the baking sheets before serving. The granola will keep in an airtight container for up to 1 month.

breakfasts

This muesli is a fantastic way to heap nutrients into your diet, including omega-3 fatty acids from the hemp and pumpkin seeds.

Muesli with Summer Fruit Compôte

Makes **6 servings**   Preparation time **15 minutes**   Cooking time **35 minutes**

MUESLI:

100g/3½oz/¾ cup chopped hazelnuts

150g/5½oz/heaped 1 cup rice flakes

50g/1¾oz/scant ½ cup buckwheat flakes

50g/1¾oz/heaped ½ cup flaked almonds

50g/1¾oz/1 cup toasted coconut flakes

2½ tbsp pumpkin seeds

1 tbsp hemp seeds

150g/5½oz/heaped ¾ cup unsulphured dried
    apricots, chopped

50g/1¾oz/¼ cup dates, chopped

2 tbsp dried goji berries

soya yogurt, to serve

soya milk, to serve

SUMMER FRUIT COMPÔTE:

8 apricots, pitted and quartered

8 plums, pitted and quartered

60g/2¼oz/⅓ cup fruit sugar or
    caster sugar

150g/5½oz/1 cup blueberries

400g/14oz/2⅔ cups strawberries, hulled

1   Preheat the oven to 180°C/350°F/gas 4. To make the compôte, put the apricots and plums in a medium-sized baking dish, sprinkle the sugar over them and bake for 10 minutes. Gently stir in the blueberries and strawberries and bake for another 25 minutes until tender. Remove from the oven and leave to cool. Store in the fridge for up to 3 days before serving.

2   To make the muesli, mix all of the ingredients together in a large mixing bowl.

3   Serve the muesli with the compôte and with soya yogurt and soya milk, if you like. The muesli will keep in an airtight container for up to 1 month.

Classic ingredients combine here to make an extremely moreish dish that is perfect for a fill-you-up breakfast or brunch.

Spanish-Style Eggs

Serves **4**   Preparation time **10 minutes**   Cooking time **35 minutes**

3 tbsp olive oil

4 potatoes, cut into small chunks

1 large sweet or mild onion, chopped

2 red peppers, deseeded and sliced

2 tbsp tomato purée

8 tomatoes, chopped

100ml/3½fl oz/scant ½ cup Vegetable Stock
   (see page 21) or vegetable stock made from
   gluten- and dairy-free stock powder

8 slices of Serrano ham or Parma ham, chopped

1 handful of chopped flat-leaf parsley leaves

4 eggs

sea salt and freshly ground black pepper

1   Heat the oil in a large, heavy-based frying pan and cook the potatoes over a medium heat for 8–10 minutes until starting to turn golden brown. Remove from the pan, using a slotted spoon, and transfer to a plate.

2   Add the onion to the pan and cook, stirring frequently, for 2–3 minutes until just starting to turn golden. Add the peppers and cook, stirring frequently, for another 2–3 minutes, then stir in the tomato purée and season lightly with salt.

3   Add the tomatoes and stock and cook, covered, over a low heat for 10 minutes, or until the potatoes are tender. Stir occasionally and add a little more stock if necessary. Gently stir in the ham and parsley.

4   With the back of a spoon, make 4 deep holes in the mixture and crack an egg into each hole. Cover again and cook for 8–10 minutes until the egg whites are cooked through. Serve immediately.

Lunches

Trying to buy a gluten-and dairy-free lunch can often be a nightmare, and, even if you do find something, it's never as good as your own home-made food. Here you'll find nutritious meals you can eat at your desk, in the park, on the beach or round your table at home. Take Tuna, Avocado and Tomato Salsa Wraps to work, for example, or Prawn, Broad Bean and Avocado Bruschetta or Tomato Tart for a picnic in the sunshine. Put a smile on your kids' faces with Chicken and Sesame Nuggets or Chargrilled Pepper, Parma Ham and Pine Nut Pizza; or make Spicy Pork Noodles or Crayfish and Asparagus Pasta for a delicious treat in the middle of the day.

Crayfish and Asparagus Pasta, page 65 >

There's something very heartwarming about soup – and chicken soup in particular. This one is full of Asian flavours, with a kick from the chilli.

Chicken and Coconut Soup

Serves **4**   Preparation time **15 minutes**   Cooking time **15 minutes**

2 lemongrass sticks, cut into thirds and bashed

2.5cm/1in piece of root ginger, peeled and
   coarsely chopped

1 red chilli, deseeded and coarsely chopped

2 shallots, coarsely chopped

2 kaffir lime leaves

1l/35fl oz/4 cups Chicken Stock (see page 20)
   or stock made from gluten- and dairy-free
   stock powder

400ml/14fl oz/scant 1⅔ cups coconut milk

2 boneless, skinless chicken breasts, sliced
   into strips

200g/7oz mushrooms, chopped

2 tbsp Thai fish sauce

juice of ½ lime

1 large handful of coriander leaves, chopped,
   to serve

1   Put the lemongrass, ginger, chilli and shallots in a mini food processor or spice mill. Pulse until finely chopped and the mixture forms a paste.

2   Put the paste in a large, heavy-based saucepan and add the kaffir lime leaves, chicken stock and coconut milk. Bring to the boil over a high heat and add the chicken, mushrooms and fish sauce. Simmer over a medium heat for 10 minutes or until the chicken is tender yet cooked through. To test that the chicken is cooked, remove a slice, prick with the tip of a sharp knife and check that the juice that runs out of it is clear, not pink.

3   Stir in the lime juice and serve immediately, sprinkled with the coriander leaves.

Mint and asparagus are a delicious combination – and the medicinal qualities of mint can aid digestion and help digestive problems and IBS.

Asparagus Soup with Mint Pesto

Serves **4**   Preparation time **15 minutes**   Cooking time **30 minutes**

1 tbsp olive oil

3 shallots, chopped

700g/1lb 9oz asparagus, woody ends removed
    and stalks roughly chopped

1l/35fl oz/4 cups Vegetable Stock (see page 21)
    or vegetable stock made from gluten- and
    dairy-free stock powder

6 large mint leaves, coarsely chopped

sea salt and freshly ground black pepper

MINT PESTO:

100g/3½oz/5 cups mint leaves, plus extra
    to decorate

50g/1¾oz/⅓ cup pine nuts

2 garlic cloves

4 tbsp olive oil

sea salt

1   Heat the oil in a large, heavy-based saucepan over a low heat. Add the shallots and cook, stirring occasionally, for 2–3 minutes until golden. Stir in the asparagus and cook, stirring occasionally, for 3–4 minutes until starting to soften.

2   Add the stock and chopped mint leaves and season lightly with salt and pepper. Bring to the boil over a high heat, then turn the heat down to low and simmer, covered, for 15–20 minutes.

3   Meanwhile, make the pesto. Rinse and carefully pat the mint dry in a clean tea towel. Heat a dry, heavy-based frying pan over a medium heat. Add the pine nuts and cook, stirring frequently, until just starting to turn golden. Remove from the heat and transfer to a food processor.

4   Add the mint leaves and garlic and start to blend. With the motor running, add the oil and blend until the mixture forms a thick, dense sauce. Transfer to a bowl and season with salt to taste.

5   Blend the soup until smooth. Stir in a large spoonful of the pesto, sprinkle with mint leaves and serve. The remaining pesto will keep in the fridge for 1–2 days, or in the freezer for up to 3 months.

lunches

Mushrooms always conjure up lovely memories of picking them with my father when I was young. Here I've used both fresh and dried ones for a richer flavour, as well as hazelnuts to add creamy thickness to the soup.

Wild Mushroom and Hazelnut Cream Soup

Serves 4   Preparation time 35 minutes, plus at least 12 hours soaking   Cooking time 30 minutes

50g/1¾oz/heaped ⅓ cup blanched hazelnuts

20g/¾oz dried porcini mushrooms

2 tbsp olive oil

1 onion, chopped

2 garlic cloves, crushed

450g/1lb mixed wild mushrooms, such as
chanterelle, porcini and oyster, washed
and sliced

250ml/9fl oz/1 cup Vegetable Stock
(see page 21) or vegetable stock made from
gluten- and dairy-free stock powder

1 handful of parsley leaves, chopped

sea salt and freshly ground black pepper

1   Put the hazelnuts in a bowl, cover with cold water and leave to soak overnight or for at least 12 hours, then drain and rinse well.

2   Put the dried mushrooms in a bowl and cover with 500ml/17fl oz/2 cups boiling water. Leave to soak for 20 minutes, then remove, using a slotted spoon, and set aside. Strain the liquid into a clean bowl and set aside.

3   Heat the oil in a large, heavy-based saucepan over a low heat. Add the onion and cook, stirring occasionally, for 2–3 minutes until golden, then add the garlic and cook, stirring, for another 30 seconds. Gently stir in the mushrooms and cook for 3–4 minutes, continuing to stir occasionally. Add the stock and reserved mushroom liquid and season lightly with salt and pepper. Bring to the boil over a high heat, then turn the heat down to low and simmer, covered, for 15–20 minutes. Stir in the parsley and simmer for another 2 minutes.

4   Meanwhile, put the hazelnuts in a food processor or blender and add 80ml/2½fl oz/⅓ cup water. Blend for 10 minutes or until very smooth. Transfer to a small bowl.

5   Blend the soup until smooth. Serve with a spoonful of the hazelnut cream stirred in. The remaining hazelnut cream will keep in the fridge for up to 3 days, or in the freezer for up to 3 months.

Sesame seeds are a great alternative to breadcrumbs. They are exceptionally high in calcium, making these nuggets a super-healthy option for kids.

Chicken Sesame Nuggets

Serves **4**   Preparation time **15 minutes, plus at least 2 hours marinating**   Cooking time **20 minutes**

4 skinless, boneless chicken breasts, sliced into
    short strips
150g/5½oz/1 cup sesame seeds

MARINADE:
125ml/4fl oz/½ cup clear honey
2 tbsp tamari soy sauce
16 spring onions, finely sliced
5cm/2in piece of root ginger, peeled and
    finely chopped

1   Put the chicken in a non-reactive baking dish. Mix together all of the ingredients for the marinade in a bowl and pour the mixture over the chicken. Cover and leave to marinate in the fridge for 2–3 hours or overnight.

2   Preheat the oven to 180°C/350°F/gas 4 and line two baking trays with baking parchment. Put the sesame seeds in a sandwich bag, remove the chicken pieces from the marinade and put them in the bag. Gently shake until all of the pieces are covered in seeds. Put the chicken on the baking trays and discard any remaining seeds.

3   Put the dish with the marinade in the oven, uncovered, along with the chicken. Bake for 15–20 minutes until the chicken is cooked through. Serve with a little of the marinade sauce poured over the nuggets.

lunches

Lentils are a storecupboard essential that provides a great source of sustained energy. Combined with the delicious aromas and flavours from the rosemary, garlic, pancetta and chicken here, they make a gorgeous meal.

Rosemary Chicken Skewers with Puy Lentils

Serves **4**   Preparation time **30 minutes, plus at least 12 hours soaking and 1 hour marinating**
Cooking time **55 minutes**

200g/7oz/1 cup Puy lentils

2 garlic cloves, peeled but left whole, plus
    1 crushed

4 tbsp olive oil

2 large skinless, boneless chicken breasts,
    cut into bite-sized pieces

125g/4½oz pancetta

3 shallots, finely chopped

600ml/21fl oz/scant 2½ cups Chicken Stock
    (see page 20) or stock made from gluten-
    and dairy-free powder

4 large rosemary sprigs, lower leaves removed

sea salt and freshly ground black pepper

1   Rinse the lentils thoroughly and put them in a large bowl. Cover with water and leave to soak overnight or for at least 12 hours, then drain, rinse well and drain again.

2   Put the whole garlic and 3 tablespoons of the oil in a mini food processor or spice mill and blend for 2–3 minutes until smooth and thick. Put the chicken in a shallow dish, pour the garlic mixture over the top and stir well to coat the chicken pieces. Cover and leave to marinate in the fridge for 1 hour or until needed.

3   Heat the remaining oil in a frying pan over a medium heat. Add the pancetta and fry for 5–6 minutes until crispy. Using a slotted spoon, transfer the pancetta to a heavy-bottomed saucepan and set aside. Add the shallots to the frying pan and fry, stirring occasionally, for 2 minutes or until starting to turn golden, then add the crushed garlic and fry for another 30 seconds. Add the mixture to the saucepan, along with all the fat from the frying pan, then add the lentils and stock. Bring to the boil over a high heat, then turn the heat down to low and simmer, covered, for 45 minutes until soft. When cooked, drain off any excess liquid and season with salt and pepper.

4   Meanwhile, soak the rosemary sprigs in cold water for 20 minutes and preheat the grill to high. Thread the chicken pieces onto the rosemary sprigs and put on a grill pan. When the lentils have been cooking for about 25 minutes, grill the skewers for 20 minutes, turning every 5 minutes, until evenly cooked through and lightly browned. Serve with the lentils.

A very simple summery salad – but full of freshness from the herbs, sweetness from the mango and deep rich flavour from the balsamic vinegar.

Chicken and Mango Salad

Serves **4**   Preparation time **15 minutes**   Cooking time **25 minutes**

4 skinless, boneless chicken breasts

5 tbsp olive oil

2 mangoes

4 avocados, peeled, pitted and sliced

12 spring onions, finely sliced

4 Little Gem lettuces, leaves separated

1 handful of basil leaves, chopped

1 handful of mint leaves, chopped

4 tbsp balsamic vinegar

1   Preheat the oven to 180°C/350°F/gas 4. Put the chicken breasts in a baking dish, drizzle with 1 tablespoon of the oil and cover. Bake for 20–25 minutes until cooked through. To test that the chicken is cooked, prick with the tip of a sharp knife and check that the juice that runs out of it is clear, not pink. Remove from the oven and leave to cool completely.

2   Using a sharp knife, carefully slice the mangoes down both sides, avoiding the stone. On the inside of each slice, cut the flesh into slices, cutting down to the peel but not piercing it, then carefully scoop out with a spoon. Peel the remaining parts of the mangoes and cut the flesh off the stones in slices. Put the mango in a large salad bowl and add the avocados, spring onions, lettuces and herbs.

3   Either chop or tear the cooled chicken into bite-sized pieces and add it to the bowl. Drizzle with the vinegar and remaining oil and toss gently but thoroughly. Serve immediately.

lunches

A nutrient-dense dish that's bursting with antioxidants, beta-carotene, vitamins and minerals, as well as full-on flavours. Here I've used rice noodles, but you could also use glass noodles instead.

Spicy Pork Noodles

Serves **4**   Preparation time **20 minutes, plus 30 minutes marinating**   Cooking time **15 minutes**

600g/1lb 5oz pork fillet, cut into strips

250g/9oz rice noodles

6 spring onions, white part only, finely sliced

200g/7oz/2 cups sugar snap peas

400g/14oz/4 cups bean sprouts

1 red pepper, deseeded and sliced

1 yellow pepper, deseeded and sliced

1 pak choi, cut into thirds, stems and leaves
    separated

50g/1¾oz/⅓ cup sesame seeds, to serve

1 handful of coriander leaves, chopped, to serve

MARINADE:

2 garlic cloves

1 red chilli, deseeded and cut into large pieces

2 lemongrass stalks, cut into large pieces

1 tbsp toasted sesame oil

1 tbsp olive oil

2 tbsp tamari soy sauce

1 tbsp Thai fish sauce

1 tbsp rice wine vinegar

1 tbsp agave syrup

1 tbsp Chinese five-spice powder

1   To make the marinade, put the garlic, chilli and lemongrass in a mini food processor or spice mill and blend until finely chopped. Put the mixture and the remaining ingredients for the marinade in a shallow non-reactive bowl and mix well. Add the pork to the marinade and stir well, making sure the pork is covered in the marinade. Cover and chill in the fridge for at least 30 minutes, or overnight.

2   Put the noodles in a large heatproof bowl, cover with boiling water and leave to stand for 5 minutes or until soft. Drain well.

3   Heat a wok or large frying pan over a high heat. Add the pork, marinade and spring onions and stir-fry for 5 minutes, then add the sugar snap peas, bean sprouts, peppers and pak choi stems. Stir-fry for another 5 minutes, then add the pak choi leaves. Stir-fry for another 2–3 minutes until the pork is cooked through and the vegetables are cooked but still slightly crunchy. Stir in the noodles and serve sprinkled with the sesame seeds and coriander leaves.

This is a fantastically versatile dish. You can eat it hot at home or pack it up into a chilled lunchbox for work or a picnic.

Spinach and Parma Ham Tortilla

Serves **4**   Preparation time **15 minutes**   Cooking time **30 minutes**

250ml/9fl oz/1 cup olive oil

2 large potatoes, thinly sliced

1 large sweet or mild onion, finely chopped

2 garlic cloves, crushed

8 slices of Parma ham, chopped

200g/7oz spinach leaves, chopped

6 large eggs

200g/7oz uncooked prawns

sea salt and freshly ground black pepper

1   Heat the oil in a large, non-stick frying pan over a medium heat. Add half of the potato slices and cook, stirring occasionally, for 5–6 minutes until soft and starting to turn golden brown. Remove from the pan, using a slotted spoon, set aside and repeat with the remaining potato slices.

2   Add the onion to the oil and cook, stirring occasionally, for 2–3 minutes until starting to turn golden. Add the garlic and fry for 30 seconds, then remove the mixture from the pan, using a slotted spoon, and discard the oil. Return the onion and garlic mixture to the pan and add the Parma ham and spinach. Cook, stirring frequently, for 2 minutes until the spinach starts to wilt.

3   Beat the eggs together in a bowl and season lightly with salt and pepper. Add the prawns and the potatoes to the frying pan and pour in the egg mixture. Stir gently to mix well, then cook for about 10 minutes until the tortilla turns golden on the bottom. Remove the pan from the heat, hold a large plate upside-down over the pan and turn the pan over so the tortilla falls out onto the plate. Slide the inverted tortilla back into the frying pan and cook the other side for 5 minutes, or until golden brown on the bottom. Serve warm.

Thought you couldn't eat pizza? Think again! This gluten-free and dairy-free pizza has a thick crust that is deliciously crunchy and crispy on the edges.

Chargrilled Pepper, Parma Ham and Pine Nut Pizza

Serves **2**   Preparation time **25 minutes, plus 30 minutes rising**   Cooking time **15 minutes**

6 tbsp passata

2 tbsp tomato purée

80g/2¾oz/1 cup drained, bottled or tinned
    chargrilled peppers in oil, cut into strips

50g/1¾oz Parma ham, thinly sliced

10 cherry tomatoes, halved

10 large basil leaves, torn into little pieces

30–60g/1–2¼oz/⅓–⅔ cup soya cheese, shaved

25g/1oz pine nuts, toasted

PIZZA DOUGH:

85g/3oz/scant ½ cup brown rice flour,
    plus extra for rolling the dough

85g/3oz/¾ cup gram flour

30g/1¼oz/¼ cup maize flour

scant ½ tsp xanthan gum

½ tsp salt

1 tsp dried active yeast

2 tbsp olive oil

1   To make the pizza dough, sift the flours, xanthan gum, salt and yeast into a large mixing bowl and, using a metal whisk, mix thoroughly. Add the oil and mix in gently. Pour in 100ml/3½fl oz/scant ½ cup warm water and, using either a wooden spoon or your hands, mix thoroughly. It will be sticky. Alternatively, sift the flours, xanthan gum, salt and yeast into a food processor. Blend to mix together, then add the oil and blend well. Add 100ml/3½fl oz/scant ½ cup warm water, a little at a time, and continue blending to form a soft dough. Process for 3–4 minutes to aerate the dough. Put the dough in a clean bowl, cover with cling film and leave to stand at room temperature for 30 minutes.

2   Preheat the oven to 220°C/425°F/gas 7 and line a baking sheet with baking parchment. Turn the dough out again onto a lightly floured surface and knead a little, then shape it into a ball. Flatten the dough slightly, roll it out into a large circle about 5mm/¼in thick and neaten the edge, using a sharp knife. Transfer the dough to the baking sheet.

3   Put the passata and tomato purée in a bowl and mix well, then spread it over the pizza base and place the peppers, ham, cherry tomatoes and basil over the top. Bake for 12 minutes until the base is starting to turn brown and the tomato sauce is bubbling. Remove the pizza from the oven and sprinkle the cheese and pine nuts over the top, then return to the oven for 3–4 minutes until the cheese has started to melt. Serve immediately.

Ume plum seasoning, made from umeboshi plums, has a zesty flavour that's a wonderful alternative to citrus or vinegar. Here it gives a sharp, tangy flavour to the noodles and beef salad.

Asian Beef Salad with Glass Noodles

Serves **4**   Preparation time **25 minutes**   Cooking time **5 minutes**

200g/7oz dried glass noodles
   (mung bean vermicelli)

1 tbsp olive oil

2 large sirloin steaks

1 large handful of coriander leaves, chopped

1 handful of mint leaves, chopped

1 cucumber, cut into matchsticks

3 carrots, cut into matchsticks

12 spring onions, white part only, finely sliced

2 Little Gem lettuces, torn into bite-sized pieces

sea salt

100g/3½oz/⅔ cup peanuts, chopped, to serve

UME PLUM DRESSING:

2 chillies, deseeded and chopped into
   large chunks

2 garlic cloves, crushed

juice of 1 lime

2 tbsp agave syrup

2 tbsp ume plum seasoning

2 tbsp Thai fish sauce

3 tbsp olive oil

1   To make the dressing, put the chillies in a mini food processor or spice mill and blend until finely chopped. Transfer to a jug and add all of the remaining ingredients for the dressing. Whisk together and set aside.

2   Put the glass noodles in a large heatproof bowl, cover with boiling water and leave to stand for 5 minutes or until translucent. Drain well.

3   Heat the oil in a frying pan or griddle pan over a medium heat. Season the steaks lightly with salt and fry for 2 minutes on each side or until browned on the outside but still pink in the middle. Slice each steak into strips and put them in a large salad bowl. Add the noodles and all of the remaining ingredients except the peanuts. Pour the dressing over the salad and toss well. Sprinkle with the peanuts and serve.

Tuna is a brilliant source of omega-3 fats. Here it's served with an avocado and tomato salsa and wrapped in warm tortillas. You'll never want to go back to dull, dry sandwiches again!

Tuna, Avocado and Tomato Salsa Wraps

Serves 4   Preparation time **15 minutes, plus making the tortillas**   Cooking time **5 minutes**

4 tomatoes, diced

6 spring onions, finely sliced

1 large red chilli, deseeded and finely chopped

1 large handful of coriander leaves, chopped

juice of 1 lime

3 avocados, peeled, pitted and roughly mashed

4 tuna steaks

1 tbsp olive oil

1 recipe quantity warm Corn Tortillas (see page 17)

8 large spinach leaves

sea salt

1   To make the salsa, mix the tomatoes, spring onions, chilli, coriander leaves and lime juice together in a large bowl and set aside. Season the avocado lightly with salt.

2   Heat a frying pan or griddle pan over a high heat. Brush the tuna lightly on each side with the oil, season lightly with salt and cook for 2–3 minutes on each side until brown on the outside but slightly pink in the middle. Remove from the pan and leave to rest for 2–3 minutes, then slice into thin strips.

3   Spread a couple spoonfuls of avocado down the middle of each tortilla. Cover with 1 spinach leaf, a few tuna strips and a couple spoonfuls of the salsa mixture. Roll up the tortillas, using baking parchment to hold the tortilla firm, and cut each one in half diagonally. Use cocktails sticks to secure the tortillas, if necessary, and serve.

lunches

Cornflour is a gem of an ingredient. You can use it to thicken sauces and desserts and combine it with spices to make a delicious coating for fish and seafood, especially the squid in this recipe.

Salt and Pepper Squid

Serves **4**   Preparation time **15 minutes**   Cooking time **15 minutes**

400g/14oz cleaned baby squid

1 tsp Sichuan peppercorns

1 tsp sea salt

¼ tsp Chinese five-spice powder

4 tbsp cornflour

500ml/17fl oz/2 cups rapeseed oil

lime wedges, to serve

DIPPING SAUCE:

1cm/½in piece of root ginger, peeled and
    coarsely chopped

1 red chilli, deseeded and coarsely chopped

1 tbsp Thai fish sauce

1 tbsp tamari soy sauce

2 tbsp clear honey

juice of 1 lime

1 small handful of coriander leaves

1 Put all of the ingredients for the dipping sauce in a mini food processor or spice mill and blend until smooth.

2 Cut the tentacles off the squid and set aside. Using a sharp knife, cut down one side of the squid tubes and open out flat. Score on the inside with a diamond pattern and pat the tubes and tentacles dry with kitchen paper.

3 Heat a dry, heavy-based frying pan over a low heat. Add the Sichuan peppercorns and cook for 2–3 minutes until slightly browned, stirring continuously so they do not burn. Remove from the heat and transfer to a mini food processor or spice mill. Add the salt and grind to a fine powder, then transfer to a small bowl and stir in the five-spice powder and cornflour.

4 Dip the squid tubes and tentacles in the flour mixture, coating them well, then put them on a plate.

5 Heat the oil in a deep frying pan or wok over a high heat until very hot. Working in batches to avoid overcrowding the pan, deep-fry the squid for 3 minutes or until lightly golden. Remove from the oil, using a slotted spoon, and drain on kitchen paper. Serve immediately with the dipping sauce.

lunches

My husband loves this! The clean sharp tastes of the chilli and lemon combine with the herbs and seafood to make a seriously good dish.

Crayfish and Asparagus Pasta

Serves **4**   Preparation time **15 minutes**   Cooking time **15 minutes**

2 shallots, halved

1 red chilli, halved and deseeded

2 garlic cloves

3 strips of lemon zest

7 tbsp olive oil

350g/12oz gluten-free pasta

350g/12oz asparagus, woody ends removed and
   stalks cut into thirds

100ml/3½fl oz/scant ½ cup Fish Stock
   (see page 20) or stock made from
   gluten- and dairy-free stock powder

350g/12oz crayfish tails

1 large handful of flat-leaf parsley leaves,
   chopped

juice of ½ lemon, plus lemon quarters to serve

sea salt and freshly ground black pepper

1   Put the shallots, chilli, garlic and lemon zest in a mini food processor or spice mill and blend until finely chopped, making sure the zest is coarsely chopped.

2   Bring a large saucepan of water to the boil and stir in 1 tablespoon of the oil. Add the pasta and cook over a medium heat for 8–10 minutes, or according to the instructions on the packet, until soft. Make sure you stir occasionally to ensure the pasta doesn't stick. Drain and rinse well with freshly boiled water, then drain again.

3   Meanwhile, in a large, heavy-bottomed saucepan, heat 4 tablespoons of the remaining oil over a medium heat. Add the shallot mixture and fry, stirring, for about 1 minute until starting to turn golden. Add the asparagus and stir well. Fry for another minute, then add the fish stock. Cook, covered, for 4 minutes, then add the crayfish. Cook for another 2 minutes until the asparagus is tender but still slightly crunchy.

4   Add the cooked pasta to the saucepan and mix well. Add the parsley, lemon juice and the remaining 2 tablespoons of olive oil. Season with salt and pepper and serve immediately with lemon quarters for squeezing over.

Make the most of delicious, fresh broad beans when you can. If they're not available, though, you could either use frozen broad beans or edamame beans.

Prawn, Broad Bean and Avocado Bruschetta

Serves **4**   Preparation time **15 minutes, plus making the bread**   Cooking time **5 minutes**

1kg/2lb 4oz fresh broad beans, podded
  (or 200g/7oz/about 1½ cups frozen)

1 avocado

350g/12oz cooked prawns, chopped

1 tbsp finely chopped mint leaves, plus a few
  mint sprigs for cooking

1 tbsp finely chopped basil leaves

1 small handful of coriander leaves,
  finely chopped

1 tbsp lime juice

2 tbsp olive oil

scant ½ tsp crushed chilli flakes

2–3 garlic cloves, peeled

12–16 slices of White Bread (see page 14),
  toasted

sea salt

1   Put the beans and mint sprigs in a steamer and steam, covered, over a high heat for 4–5 minutes until tender. Remove and discard the mint.

2   Rinse the beans under cold running water, then drain well and transfer to a bowl. Remove and discard the skins from the beans by squeezing the skins until they pop out. Mash the beans coarsely. Peel the avocado, remove and discard the stone, then mash the flesh coarsely and stir it into the beans. Add the prawns, chopped herbs, lime juice, olive oil and chilli flakes and mix well. Season to taste with salt.

3   Rub the garlic onto the toasted bread slices and top with a spoonful of the prawn mixture. Serve immediately.

lunches

Quinoa contains all eight essential amino acids, as well as high quantities of calcium and magnesium, so it's wonderful to include in your repertoire. Frying the quinoa before adding the water enhances the taste and texture.

Roasted Vegetables and Quinoa

Serves **4**   Preparation time **15 minutes**   Cooking time **45 minutes**

20 small carrots

10 small beetroot, halved

3 fennel bulbs, fronds removed, and quartered

2 aubergines, quartered

2 red peppers, deseeded and quartered

125ml/4fl oz/½ cup olive oil

1 large onion, chopped

300g/10½oz/1½ cups quinoa

2 tsp ground cumin

2 tsp ground coriander

juice of 1 lemon

1 large handful of coriander leaves, chopped

1 large handful of flat-leaf parsley leaves, chopped

sea salt

1   Preheat the oven to 180°C/350°F/gas 4. Put the carrots and beetroot in a large roasting tin, and the fennel, aubergines and peppers in another large roasting tin. Drizzle half of the oil into the two tins and toss well to coat. First bake the carrots and beetroot for 10 minutes, then put the other roasting tin in the oven and bake both for another 30–35 minutes or until all of the vegetables are slightly browned and tender.

2   Meanwhile, heat the remaining olive oil in a saucepan over a medium heat. Add the onion and cook, stirring occasionally, for 2 minutes. Add the quinoa and cook, stirring occasionally, for another 4–5 minutes until evenly browned. Add 600ml/21fl oz/scant 2½ cups water and bring to the boil over a high heat. Reduce the heat to low and simmer for 20 minutes or until tender, adding a little extra water if necessary.

3   Mix the vegetables and quinoa together in a large bowl and add the cumin, ground coriander, lemon juice and coriander and parsley leaves. Season with salt and serve either hot or cold.

There's something truly lovely about eating a good gluten- and dairy-free version of a classic recipe. Here I've added fried courgettes for toasted sweet flavours and strongly aromatic sage to make a truly comforting meal.

Courgette and Sage Spaghetti Carbonara

Serves **4**   Preparation time **15 minutes**   Cooking time **25 minutes**

125ml/4fl oz/½ cup olive oil

2 courgettes, trimmed, halved and shaved into ribbons, using a vegetable peeler

400g/14oz gluten-free spaghetti

300g/10½oz pancetta

1 heaped tbsp chopped sage leaves

4 large egg yolks

80ml/2½fl oz/⅓ cup soya cream

200g/7oz/2 cups soya cheese, grated

sea salt and freshly ground black pepper

1 Heat 6 tablespoons of the oil in a wok or large frying pan over a medium heat. Working in batches, add a large handful of the courgette ribbons and fry, stirring occasionally, for 5–6 minutes until soft and lightly browned. With a slotted spoon, remove the courgette from the pan and set aside.

2 Bring a large saucepan of water to the boil. Add 1 tablespoon of the remaining oil, then the spaghetti, pushing it down into the water as it softens. Cook over a medium-high heat for 8–10 minutes, or according to the packet instructions, stirring frequently to make sure the spaghetti doesn't stick together.

3 Meanwhile, heat the remaining tablespoon of the oil in a frying pan over a medium heat. Add the pancetta and fry, stirring occasionally, for 5–6 minutes until crispy. Remove the pancetta from the pan, using a slotted spoon, and set aside. Add the sage and fry for 1–2 minutes until crispy. Set aside, reserving the fat in the pan.

4 In a medium bowl, whisk together the egg yolks and soya cream, then whisk in the soya cheese and set aside.

5 Drain the spaghetti and rinse well with boiling water, then drain again briefly, leaving a little of the water remaining. Put the spaghetti back in the saucepan and quickly stir in the egg mixture. Quickly add the courgette, pancetta and sage, along with all of the fat remaining in the pan. Stir well and season with salt and pepper, then serve immediately.

I love baking – when I open the door of the oven and take out the finished result, it feels like I've created something wonderful. This tart is brimming with the beautiful tastes and fresh aromas of summertime.

Tomato Tart

Serves **4**   Preparation time **5 minutes, plus making the pastry**   Cooking time **50 minutes**

dairy-free margarine, for greasing

2 aubergines

1 recipe quantity Light Pastry (see page 18)

brown rice flour, for rolling the pastry

100g/3½oz sun-dried tomato paste

6–7 tomatoes, sliced and end pieces discarded

12 cherry tomatoes, cut in half lengthways

1 small handful of basil leaves, finely chopped

sea salt and freshly ground black pepper

1   Preheat the oven to 200°C/400°F/gas 6 and grease a loose-based, 20 x 30cm/8 x 12in tart tin with dairy-free margarine. Prick the aubergines all over with a fork, put them in a baking tray and bake for 45 minutes until very soft.

2   Meanwhile, liberally dust a large chopping board with rice flour and gently roll out the pastry to about 5mm/¼in thick. Put the loose base of the tart tin on top of the pastry and, using a sharp knife, cut around it. Shape the pastry trimmings into a ball and set aside. Lift the chopping board and turn it over to drop the pastry and base into the tin.

3   Dust the chopping board again with rice flour and gently roll the remaining pastry out again. Cut it into strips wide enough to line the sides of the tin. To secure the sides of the tart, lightly brush some water along the bottom edges of the pastry strips that will overlap with the base. Gently press the pastry into the sides of the tin and along the bottom edge where it overlaps with the pastry on the base, taking care to remove any air pockets. Neaten the edges, using a sharp knife, then prick the bottom of the pastry with a fork. Line the pastry case with a piece of baking parchment and fill with baking beans. Bake alongside the aubergines for 15 minutes until lightly golden. Take the pastry case out of the oven and remove the parchment and beans, then bake for another 2–3 minutes.

4   Remove the aubergines from the oven and turn the oven down to 180°C/350°F/gas 4. Cut the aubergines in half and, using a spoon, scoop the flesh into a bowl. Mash well with a fork, then mix in the sun-dried tomato paste.

5   Spread the aubergine and tomato mixture over the bottom of the pastry case and cover with the sliced tomatoes, followed by the cherry tomatoes. Sprinkle with the basil and season with salt and pepper. Bake for 20–25 minutes until the pastry is golden brown. Serve either hot or cold.

Arame is my favourite sea vegetable. It has a lovely, nutty taste and an exceptional nutritional profile, providing incredible quantities of calcium, iron and magnesium, as well as phytonutrients.

Arame and Cashew Nut Stir-Fry

Serves **4**   Preparation time **15 minutes, plus 30 minutes soaking**   Cooking time **10 minutes**

20g/¾oz arame

1 tbsp kuzu

2 tbsp toasted sesame oil

2 tbsp olive oil

1 onion, finely chopped

2 garlic cloves, crushed

2.5cm/1in piece of root ginger, peeled and
    finely chopped

2 carrots, cut into matchsticks

2 yellow or orange peppers, deseeded and
    finely sliced

100g/3½oz Chinese cabbage, finely sliced

150g/5½oz mangetout

200g/7oz/2¼ cups bean sprouts

2½ tbsp tamari soy sauce, plus extra if needed

2½ tbsp rice wine vinegar

2½ tbsp agave syrup

100ml/3½fl oz/scant ½ cup Vegetable Stock
    (see page 21) or vegetable stock made from
    gluten- and dairy-free stock powder

150g/5½oz/1 cup cashew nuts

1   Soak the arame in a bowl of cold water for about 30 minutes, then drain and rinse. Meanwhile, put the kuzu and 1 tablespoon cold water in a small bowl and stir to form a smooth paste, then set aside.

2   Heat both of the oils in a wok or large frying pan over a high heat. Add the onion and stir-fry for 1 minute, then stir in the garlic and ginger. Add the carrot, pepper and cabbage and stir-fry for 2–3 minutes. Add the mangetout, bean sprouts and soaked arame and stir-fry for another 2 minutes.

3   Mix in the tamari, rice wine vinegar and agave syrup, then add the kuzu paste and stock. Cook, stirring, for another 2–3 minutes until all of the vegetables are cooked but remain quite crunchy.

4   Stir in the cashew nuts. Check the seasoning and add extra tamari if needed. Serve hot.

lunches

This collection of meze recipes makes a great lunch for friends and family, either in small or large numbers. Make everything the night before and enjoy a relaxed day!

Pomegranate Yogurt Dip

Serves **4**   Preparation time **10 minutes**   Cooking time **5 minutes**

50g/1¾oz/⅓ cup pine nuts

350g/12oz/1⅔ cups unflavoured soya yogurt

2 pomegranates

1 garlic clove, crushed

1 handful of mint leaves, chopped

1 handful of coriander leaves, chopped

sea salt

1   Heat a heavy-based frying pan over a medium heat. Add the pine nuts and cook, stirring continuously, for 3–4 minutes until just beginning to brown. Remove from the heat and set aside.

2   Whisk the yogurt in a large bowl until smooth. Halve the pomegranates and, holding each half over the bowl, bash the outer skin with a wooden spoon until all of the seeds fall into the bowl. You'll need to bash the skin a few times before the seeds begin to fall out, but they will. Add the pine nuts, garlic, mint and coriander leaves and mix well. Season lightly with salt and serve immediately or cover and keep in the fridge until needed.

Aubergine Spread

Serves **4**   Preparation time **10 minutes**   Cooking time **45 minutes**

2 aubergines

3 tbsp tahini

juice of 2 lemons

2 garlic cloves, crushed

2 tbsp olive oil

1 large handful of parsley leaves, chopped

1 handful of mint leaves, chopped

sea salt

1   Preheat the oven to 200°C/400°F/gas 6. Prick the aubergines all over with a fork, put them in a baking tray and bake for 45 minutes until soft. Cut in half and, using a spoon, scoop the flesh into a food processor. Add the tahini, lemon juice, garlic and oil. Season lightly with salt.

2   Blend well, then transfer to a bowl and stir in the parsley and mint. Serve immediately or cover and keep in the fridge until needed.

Fennel and Tomato Salad

Serves **4**   Preparation time **15 minutes**

2 fennel bulbs

½ cucumber, diced

½ red onion, sliced

4 tomatoes, diced

juice of 1 lemon

4 tbsp olive oil

1 large handful of coriander leaves, chopped

1 large handful of parsley leaves, chopped

sea salt

1   Trim off the leafy fronds at the top of the fennel and put them in a salad bowl. Slice the fennel bulbs in half lengthways, then slice thinly and add to the bowl. Add all of the remaining ingredients and stir well.

2   Season lightly with salt and serve immediately or cover and keep in the fridge until needed.

Cannellini Bean Dip

Serves **4**   Preparation time **10 minutes, plus at least 12 hours soaking (optional)**
Cooking time **1 hour 40 minutes**

100g/3½oz/½ cup dried cannellini beans
 or 230g/8oz/1¼ cups drained tinned
 cannellini beans, rinsed

a pinch of ground cumin

1 garlic clove, crushed

1 tbsp pomegranate molasses

1 tbsp lemon juice

scant ½ tsp harissa paste

3 tbsp olive oil

sea salt

1   If using dried cannellini beans, put them in a bowl, cover with cold water and leave to soak overnight or for at least 12 hours, then drain and rinse well. Transfer to a large saucepan, cover with fresh water and bring to the boil over a high heat. Boil for 10 minutes, then turn the heat down to medium and simmer, covered, for 1–1½ hours until tender. Drain well.

2   Put all of the ingredients in a food processor, season with salt and blend for 3–4 minutes until smooth. Leave to cool, then serve or cover and keep in the fridge until needed.

Baked Treats

Baking can be ridiculously easy – and wonderfully satisfying.
The aromas that envelop the kitchen and the creations that come
out of the oven seem almost magical. And perhaps even more so when
you're cooking without gluten or dairy. Turn the oven on, line up the
ingredients and start mixing – it's good for the soul! Dive into rich
Chocolate and Mango Florentines, sweet Apricot, Yogurt and Honey
Cake or light, fluffy Almond Cake, for example. Add another bread to
your repertoire with delicious Fruit Loaf; make a little piece of heaven
with Raspberry and Rosewater Cupcakes or Portuguese Custard Tarts;
or whip up a stunning Chocolate Birthday Cake.

Apple Cake, page 100 >

I've used figs to add moisture to these delicious cookies, hold them together and add a crunchy chewiness – but also because they make them a seriously healthy version of a chocolate cookie!

Chocolate and Fig Cookies

Makes **12**   Preparation time **15 minutes**   Cooking time **40 minutes**

150g/5½oz/1 cup dried figs, stems discarded,
    finely chopped

100g/3½oz dairy-free margarine

100g/3½oz/heaped ½ cup fruit sugar or
    caster sugar

100g/3½oz dairy-free dark chocolate,
    70% cocoa solids, broken into small pieces

1 egg, beaten

2 tsp vanilla extract

100g/3½oz/heaped ½ cup rice flour

50g/1¾oz/scant ½ cup gram flour

50g/1¾oz/⅓ cup maize flour

½ tsp gluten-free baking powder

½ tsp xanthan gum

1 Preheat the oven to 180°C/350°F/gas 4 and line two baking sheets with baking parchment. Put the figs and 350ml/12fl oz/scant 1½ cups water in a saucepan, bring to the boil over a high heat and then turn the heat down to medium. Simmer for 20 minutes, stirring occasionally, until the figs have softened and the water has been absorbed.

2 Meanwhile, put the dairy-free margarine and sugar in a saucepan and heat over a low heat until the dairy-free margarine has melted and the sugar has dissolved. Bring to the boil over a high heat, then turn the heat down to medium-low and simmer for 4–5 minutes until the mixture has become syrupy and slightly darker in colour.

3 When the sugar mixture has changed colour, turn the heat to low and add the chocolate. Continue simmering, stirring occasionally, until melted. Add the egg and vanilla extract and mix well. Pour the mixture into a large mixing bowl and sift in the flours, gluten-free baking powder and xanthan gum. Add the softened figs and stir well with a wooden spoon until mixed.

4 Shape 1 tablespoon of the mixture into a round with your hands and place on the baking sheet, pressing the tines of a fork gently over the surface to score lightly. Repeat with the remaining mixture to make 12 cookies.

5 Bake for 20 minutes or until lightly browned. Remove from the oven and leave to cool for 5 minutes, then transfer to a wire rack and leave to cool completely before serving.

baked treats

These biscuits were one of the things I loved when I was pregnant and suffering from morning sickness. They're very simple to make – and the ginger in them soothes digestive problems and eases nausea.

Ginger Biscuits

Makes **12**   Preparation time **15 minutes**   Cooking time **20 minutes**

175g/6oz dairy-free margarine

125g/4½oz/¾ cup fruit sugar or caster sugar

100g/3½oz/heaped ½ cup rice flour

50g/1¾oz/scant ½ cup gram flour

50g/1¾oz/⅓ cup maize flour

2 tsp ground ginger

½ tsp gluten-free baking powder

scant ½ tsp xanthan gum

1cm/½in piece of root ginger, peeled and grated

1   Preheat the oven to 180°C/350°F/gas 4 and line two baking sheets with baking parchment. Put the dairy-free margarine and sugar in a saucepan and heat over a low heat until the margarine has melted and the sugar has dissolved. Bring to the boil over a high heat, then turn the heat down to medium-low and simmer for 4–5 minutes until the mixture has caramelized slightly and become syrupy.

2   Sift the flours into a large mixing bowl and stir in the ground ginger, gluten-free baking powder and xanthan gum. Add the root ginger and, using your fingertips, rub it into the flour mixture until well mixed. Add the margarine and sugar syrup, and stir well with a wooden spoon.

3   Spoon the mixture, 1 tablespoon at a time, onto the baking sheets. Using your hands and the back of a metal spoon, shape each mound into a round biscuit shape about 3mm/⅛in thick.

4   Bake for 8–12 minutes until lightly browned. Remove from the oven and leave to cool for 5 minutes, then transfer to a wire rack and leave to cool completely before serving.

baked treats

This is a healthy twist on the classic Florentine recipe, using dried mango instead of sugar-loaded candied peel and glacé cherries.

Mango and Hazelnut Florentines

Makes **8–10**   Preparation time **15 minutes, plus 30 minutes chilling**   Cooking time **35 minutes**

100g/3½oz dried mango, chopped

75g/2½oz dairy-free margarine, plus extra
    for greasing

75g/2½oz/scant ½ cup fruit sugar or
    caster sugar

1 tbsp rice flour

1 tbsp gram flour

1 tbsp maize flour

¼ tsp xanthan gum

50g/1¾oz/heaped ⅓ cup chopped hazelnuts

100g/3½oz dairy-free dark chocolate,
    70% cocoa solids, chopped

1   Preheat the oven to 180°C/350°F/gas 4. Line two baking sheets with baking parchment and grease them with dairy-free margarine. Put the dried mango and 250ml/9fl oz/1 cup water in a saucepan. Bring to the boil over a high heat, then turn the heat down to medium and simmer for 15–20 minutes until the mango has softened and the water has been absorbed.

2   Meanwhile, put the dairy-free margarine and sugar in a saucepan and heat over a low heat until the margarine has melted and the sugar has dissolved. Bring to the boil over a high heat, then turn the heat down to medium-low and simmer for 4–5 minutes until the mixture has caramelized slightly and become syrupy.

3   Sift the flours and xanthan gum into a large mixing bowl. Add the hazelnuts, softened mango, and margarine and sugar syrup. Stir well with a wooden spoon until mixed. Spoon the mixture, 1 tablespoon at a time, onto the baking sheets to make 8–10 balls, leaving some space between each one. Press down on each mound with the back of the spoon to make a round biscuit shape, about 2mm/1⁄16in thick. Bake for 10–12 minutes until lightly browned. Remove from the oven and leave to cool for 5 minutes, then transfer to a wire rack and leave to cool completely.

4   Meanwhile, put the chocolate in a large heatproof bowl and rest it over a pan of gently simmering water, making sure that the bottom of the bowl does not touch the water. Stir occasionally until the chocolate has melted. When the biscuits have cooled, put them flat-side up on a plate and carefully spoon some of the melted chocolate on top of each one and spread it over evenly. Chill the biscuits in the fridge for 30 minutes or until the chocolate has set, then serve.

baked treats

Hemp seeds, figs, dates and pomegranate molasses provide a Moroccan twist to this gooey yet crunchy fruit and nut bar.

Fig and Date Fruit Bars

Makes **8**   Preparation time **15 minutes**   Cooking time **35 minutes**

dairy-free margarine, for greasing

200g/7oz/1¼ cups dried figs, stems discarded,
    chopped

100g/3½oz/heaped ½ cup pitted dates,
    chopped

50g/1¾oz/⅓ cup pine nuts

1 tbsp pomegranate molasses

2 tbsp agave syrup

150g/5½oz/heaped 1 cup rice flakes

1 tbsp hemp seeds

1   Preheat the oven to 180°C/350°F/gas 4. Grease two 450g/1lb loaf tins with dairy-free margarine and line the base with baking parchment. Put the figs, dates and 375ml/13fl oz/1½ cups water in a saucepan and bring to the boil over a high heat, then turn the heat down to medium and simmer for 15 minutes, or until the fruit has softened and the water has been absorbed.

2   Meanwhile, heat a heavy-based frying pan over a medium heat until hot. Add the pine nuts and heat, stirring frequently, until lightly browned, then transfer to a large mixing bowl.

3   Add the softened fruit, pomegranate molasses and agave syrup to the bowl and mix well. Add the rice flakes and stir well, using a wooden spoon. Divide the mixture evenly between the two loaf tins and level the surfaces with the back of a spoon. Sprinkle the hemp seeds over the tops and press down firmly with your fingertips.

4   Bake for 18–20 minutes until lightly browned and firm. Remove from the oven and leave to cool in the tins for 5 minutes, then cut each one into 4 bars. Gently ease them out of the tins and leave to cool completely on a wire rack before serving.

Ground almonds make these cupcakes deliciously light and moist. Covered with a thick, silky rosewater-flavoured frosting, they are truly indulgent!

Raspberry and Rosewater Cupcakes

Makes **12**   Preparation time **15 minutes**   Cooking time **25 minutes**

150g/5½oz dairy-free margarine, softened

125g/4½oz/¾ cup fruit sugar or caster sugar

3 eggs

75g/2½oz/heaped ⅓ cup rice flour

1 tsp gluten-free baking powder

scant ½ tsp xanthan gum

75g/2½oz/scant ¾ cup ground almonds

100g/3½oz/scant 1 cup raspberries, lightly
    mashed, plus 12 to decorate

ROSEWATER FROSTING:

25g/1oz dairy-free margarine

75g/2½oz/⅓ cup soya cream cheese

1 tsp rosewater

85g/3oz/½ cup fruit sugar or caster sugar

1   Preheat the oven to 180°C/350°F/gas 4 and arrange 12 paper cupcake cases in a bun tin. To make the frosting, put the dairy-free margarine, soya cream cheese and rosewater in a mixing bowl and beat, using a whisk or hand-held electric mixer, until smooth. Add the sugar, a little at a time, and beat until light and fluffy. Cover and chill in the fridge for 30 minutes.

2   Using an electric mixer, beat the dairy-free margarine and sugar together in a large mixing bowl until light and fluffy. Gradually beat in the eggs, one at a time, until well mixed.

3   Sift the rice flour, gluten-free baking powder and xanthan gum into the mixture. Quickly fold in the ground almonds, using a spoon, then gently fold in the raspberries. Mix well, but take care not to overmix. Divide the mixture evenly into the cupcake cases.

4   Bake for 18–20 minutes, until golden brown and well risen and a skewer inserted in the centre comes out clean. Remove from the oven and turn out of the tin, then transfer to a wire rack and leave to cool completely.

5   Spread a little of the frosting over each cupcake, top with a raspberry and serve.

baked treats

Nutmeg is naturally sweet and, when combined with vanilla extract, it creates a rich, warm flavour for the light, creamy filling in these tarts.

Portuguese Custard Tarts

Makes **4**   Preparation time **15 minutes, plus making the pastry**   Cooking time **35 minutes**

dairy-free margarine, for greasing

rice flour, for rolling the dough

1 recipe quantity Sweet Shortcrust Pastry
    with ½ tsp freshly grated nutmeg added
    (see page 19)

400ml/14fl oz/scant 1⅔ cups soya milk

1½ tbsp cornflour

85g/2¾oz/scant ½ cup fruit sugar or
    caster sugar

scant 1 tsp vanilla extract

1 tsp freshly grated nutmeg, plus extra
    for sprinkling

4 large egg yolks, beaten

1   Preheat the oven to 200°C/400°F/gas 6 and grease four 10cm/4in loose-based tartlet tins with dairy-free margarine. Liberally dust a work surface with rice flour and gently roll out the pastry to about 3mm/⅛in thick. Be very gentle, as the dough will still be slightly sticky. Using a pastry cutter that is slightly larger in diameter than the tartlet tins (to allow enough pastry for the sides), cut out four circles. Gather up the pastry trimmings, wrap in cling film and freeze for use another time.

2   Lift the pastry circles into each tin (you may need to use a metal spatula) and press down lightly to remove any air pockets. Neaten the edges, using a sharp knife, then line each pastry case with a piece of baking parchment, cover with baking beans and put them on a baking sheet. Bake for 8–10 minutes until firm and very lightly golden. Remove from the oven and turn the oven down to 180°C/350°F/gas 4.

3   Meanwhile, heat the soya milk in a heavy-based saucepan over a low heat until almost boiling. While the soya milk is warming, put the cornflour and 1 tablespoon water in a small bowl and stir until smooth. Whisk the paste, sugar, vanilla extract and nutmeg into the hot milk, then whisk in the egg yolks a little bit at a time until incorporated. Cook over a low heat, stirring frequently, for 10–15 minutes until the mixture forms a thick custard. Be careful not to overheat or it may curdle; if it does, beat with a whisk until smooth.

4   Remove the baking parchment and beans from the pastry cases and fill with the custard, using a small ladle. Sprinkle a little nutmeg over the tarts and bake for 15 minutes, or until set. Remove from the oven and leave to cool for 5 minutes. Lift out of the tins and either serve warm or transfer to a wire rack to cool before serving. Chill any leftover tarts.

baked treats

Soya yogurt has a delicious, tangy taste and a smooth, creamy texture when blended. Here it adds moisture and velvety thickness to the cake mixture – and makes a cool, light topping.

Apricot, Yogurt and Honey Cake

Makes **1 cake (10–12 slices)**   Preparation time **15 minutes**   Cooking time **50 minutes**

150g/5½oz dairy-free margarine, softened, plus
    extra for greasing

125g/4½oz/¾ cup fruit sugar or caster sugar

2 eggs, beaten

1 tsp vanilla extract

4 tbsp clear honey

250g/9oz/heaped cup unflavoured soya yogurt

100g/3½oz/heaped ½ cup rice flour

50g/1¾oz/scant ½ cup gram flour

50g/1¾oz/⅓ cup maize flour

2 tsp gluten-free baking powder

½ tsp xanthan gum

150g/5½oz/scant 1 cup unsulphured
    dried apricots, finely chopped

TOPPING:

100g/3½oz/½ cup unflavoured soya yogurt

2 tbsp clear honey

1   Preheat the oven to 180°C/350°F/gas 4 and lightly grease a deep 20cm/8in cake tin with dairy-free margarine and line the base with baking parchment. Using an electric mixer, beat the dairy-free margarine and sugar together in a large mixing bowl until light and fluffy. Gradually beat in the eggs, a little at a time, until well mixed, then beat in the vanilla extract, honey and soya yogurt.

2   Sift the flours, gluten-free baking powder and xanthan gum into the mixture and fold in, then fold in the chopped apricots. Make sure the mixture is well mixed, but take care not to overmix it. Pour it into the tin.

3   Bake for 30 minutes, then cover with baking parchment to prevent the cake from overbrowning. Bake for another 15–20 minutes until firm to the touch and cooked through.

4   Meanwhile, prepare the topping. Using a whisk or hand-held electric mixer, whisk the yogurt and honey together in a bowl until smooth. Keep cool in the fridge until needed.

5   Remove the cake from the oven and leave to cool for 5 minutes, then remove from the tin, transfer to a wire rack and leave to cool completely. Once cooled, spread the topping over the cake and serve. Store any leftover cake in the fridge.

Thanks to the ground almonds, this cake comes out of the oven light, fluffy and moist. The flavours are delicate, and the almond cream and flaked almonds add a rich coating with a crunchy top.

Almond Cake

Makes **1 cake (10–12 slices)**   Preparation time **20 minutes, plus at least 12 hours soaking**
Cooking time **35 minutes**

150g/5½oz **dairy-free margarine, softened, plus**
   extra for greasing
75g/2½oz/heaped ⅓ cup **fruit sugar or**
   caster sugar
1 tsp **almond extract**
3 **eggs, beaten**
175g/6oz/heaped 1⅔ cups **ground almonds**
1 tsp **gluten-free baking powder**

scant ½ tsp **xanthan gum**
30g/1oz/⅓ cup **flaked almonds, to decorate**

ALMOND CREAM:
100g/3½oz/⅔ cup **blanched almonds**
2 tbsp **fruit sugar or caster sugar**
¼ tsp **almond extract**
2 tsp **agar agar flakes**

1   To make the almond cream, put the blanched almonds in a bowl, cover with water and leave
   to soak overnight or for at least 12 hours, then drain, rinse well and transfer to a blender.
   Add 150ml/5fl oz/scant ⅔ cup water and blend for 10 minutes until smooth. Pour the
   mixture into a saucepan and add the sugar, almond extract and agar agar flakes. Heat over a
   low heat for 3–4 minutes until the sugar and agar agar flakes have dissolved completely,
   stirring continuously to make sure the mixture doesn't burn. Transfer to a heatproof bowl,
   leave to cool, then cover and chill in the fridge until needed.

2   Preheat the oven to 180°C/350°F/gas 4 and lightly grease a 20cm/8in cake tin with dairy-
   free margarine and line the base with baking parchment. Using an electric mixer, beat the
   dairy-free margarine and sugar together in a large mixing bowl until light and fluffy. Beat in
   the almond extract and gradually beat in the eggs, a little at a time, until well mixed. Add the
   ground almonds, gluten-free baking powder and xanthan gum to the mixture, then quickly
   fold in, using a spoon. Mix well, but take care not to overmix, then pour into the tin.

3   Bake for 20–25 minutes until golden brown, well risen and a skewer inserted in the centre
   comes out clean. Remove from the oven and leave to cool for 5 minutes. Turn out of the tin,
   transfer to a wire rack and leave to cool completely.

4   Spread the almond cream over the cake, sprinkle with the flaked almonds and serve. Keep
   any leftover cake in the fridge.

baked treats

I've used quinoa flour in this cake and a mixture of rice flour and ground almonds. The almonds and dried fruits sweeten and enrich the quinoa's distinctive, nutty taste.

Fruit Cake

Makes **1 cake (12–14 slices)**   Preparation time **20 minutes**   Cooking time **1 hour 25 minutes**

225g/8oz dairy-free margarine, plus extra for greasing

200g/7oz/scant 1⅔ cups raisins

200g/7oz/scant 1⅔ cups sultanas

250g/9oz/scant 2 cups unsulphured dried apricots, chopped

40g/1½oz/scant ¼ cup dried sour cherries

50g/1¾oz/ ⅓ cup dried cranberries

30g/1oz dried goji berries

125g/4½oz/scant 1 cup blanched hazelnuts

100g/3½oz/heaped ½ cup rice flour

100g/3½oz/⅔ cup quinoa flour

¼ tsp salt

2 tsp cinnamon

1½ tsp gluten-free baking powder

heaped ½ tsp xanthan gum

100g/3½oz/1 cup ground almonds

200g/7oz/heaped 1 cup fruit sugar or caster sugar

4 large eggs, beaten

1   Preheat the oven to 180°C/350°F/gas 4 and lightly grease a 23cm/9in springform cake tin with dairy-free margarine. Put the raisins, sultanas, apricots, cherries, cranberries, goji berries and 1l/35fl oz/4 cups water in a saucepan. Bring to the boil over a high heat, then turn the heat down to medium and simmer for 30–40 minutes until all of the fruit has softened and the water has been absorbed.

2   Put the hazelnuts in a mini food processor and pulse until chopped.

3   Sift the flours, salt, cinnamon, gluten-free baking powder and xanthan gum into a large mixing bowl. Add the ground almonds and mix well.

4   Using an electric mixer, beat the dairy-free margarine and sugar together in a large mixing bowl until light and fluffy. Gradually beat in the eggs, one at a time, until well mixed, then stir in the softened fruits and chopped hazelnuts, using a spoon. Quickly fold in the flour mixture. Make sure the batter is well blended, but take care not to overmix. Pour the batter into the tin and smooth the surface with the back of a metal spoon.

5   Bake for 30 minutes, then cover with baking parchment, tucking the ends under the tin securely. Bake for another 10–15 minutes until cooked through. The cake will seem very gooey when it comes out of the oven, but it will set as it cools. Leave to cool in the tin for 5 minutes, then turn out and transfer to a wire rack. Leave to cool completely before serving.

baked treats

This heavenly cake was inspired by one my sister made for her husband's
birthday. It's light and moist, with dark truffley chocolate flavours and
a rich, creamy icing, all covered with sweetly sharp raspberries.

Chocolate Birthday Cake

Makes **1 cake**   Preparation time **25 minutes, plus making the nut cream**   Cooking time **45 minutes**

150g/5½oz dairy-free margarine, softened, plus
    extra for greasing
200g/7oz dairy-free dark chocolate, 70% cocoa
    solids, chopped or broken into pieces
175g/6oz/scant 1 cup fruit sugar or caster sugar
1 tsp vanilla extract
4 large eggs
60g/2¼oz/scant ¼ cup rice flour
60g/2¼oz/⅓ cup chestnut flour
2 tsp gluten-free baking powder

½ tsp xanthan gum
150g/5½oz/1¼ cups raspberries or
    strawberries, hulled, to decorate

ICING:
200g/7oz dairy-free dark chocolate, 70% cocoa
    solids, chopped or broken into pieces
1 recipe quantity Cashew Nut Cream
    (see page 13), adding 1 tsp vanilla extract
    and 8 dates when blending

1   Preheat the oven to 180°C/350°F/gas 4 and lightly grease two 23cm/9in springform cake
tins with dairy-free margarine. Put the chocolate in a large heatproof bowl and rest it over
a pan of gently simmering water, making sure that the bottom of the bowl does not touch
the water. Heat, stirring occasionally, until the chocolate has melted.

2   Using an electric mixer, beat the dairy-free margarine and sugar together in a large mixing
bowl until light and fluffy. Beat in the vanilla extract, then beat in the eggs, one at a time.
Using a large spoon, carefully fold in the melted chocolate mixture. Sift the flours, gluten-free
baking powder and xanthan gum into the mixture and fold in. Make sure the mixture is well
mixed but take care not to overmix it. Evenly divide the mixture into the cake tins and level
the surfaces with the back of a spoon.

3   Bake for 35–40 minutes until firm to the touch and a skewer inserted in the centre comes
out clean. Remove from the oven and leave to cool in the tins for 5 minutes, then turn out
onto wire racks and leave to cool completely.

4   Meanwhile, put the chocolate for the icing in a large heatproof bowl and follow the same
procedure as in step 1, above, to melt it. Put the blended nut cream and date mixture in a
food processor or blender, add the melted chocolate and blend until well mixed.

5   Put 1 cake on a plate and spread half of the icing over the top. Put the other cake on top, flat-
side down, and spread the remaining icing over it. Decorate with the raspberries and serve.

This recipe is my homage to Dorset, where I grew up. The sweet flavours and soft texture of the apples combine beautifully with the firm cake base.

Apple Cake

Makes **1 cake (10–12 slices)**   Preparation time **20 minutes**   Cooking time **50 minutes**

155g/5½oz dairy-free margarine, softened, plus
    extra for greasing
4 apples, peeled, cored and cut into large chunks
4 tbsp agave syrup
125g/4½oz/¾ cup fruit sugar or caster sugar
1 tsp vanilla extract

3 large eggs
100g/3½oz/heaped ½ cup rice flour
50g/1¾oz/scant ½ cup gram flour
1 tsp gluten-free baking powder
½ tsp xanthan gum
50g/1¾oz/scant ½ cup ground almonds

1   Preheat the oven to 180°C/350°F/gas 4. Lightly grease a deep 20cm/8in cake tin with dairy-free margarine and line the base with baking parchment. Heat 15g/½oz of the dairy-free margarine in a heavy-based saucepan over a gentle heat, then add the apples and cook for 5 minutes until starting to brown, shaking the pan or gently stirring occasionally so they do not burn. Add the agave syrup and cook for another 5 minutes until soft, shaking the pan occasionally, then set aside.

2   Meanwhile, using an electric mixer, beat the sugar and remaining dairy-free margarine together in a large mixing bowl until light and fluffy. Add the vanilla extract, then gradually beat in the eggs, one at a time, until well mixed.

3   Sift the flours, gluten-free baking powder and xanthan gum into the mixture. Add the ground almonds and fold together, using a spoon. Make sure the mixture is well mixed, but take care not to overmix. Pour it into the tin and level the surface, using a clean knife. Arrange the apples on top (use the back of a spoon to even them, if needed) and pour the syrup from the pan evenly over the top. Bake for 40 minutes until firm to the touch and cooked through.

4   Remove from the oven and leave to cool for 5 minutes, then turn out of the pan and transfer to a wire rack. Leave to cool completely before serving.

baked treats

Unlike most gluten-free flours, chestnut flour has great binding properties, so it's a wonderful choice for baking. Its distinctive taste can sometimes overpower others, but the sultanas and raisins here complement it.

Fruit Loaf

Makes **1 loaf (about 16 slices)**   Preparation time **20 minutes, plus 30 minutes rising**
Cooking time **1 hour 10 minutes**

100g/3½oz/heaped ¾ cup sultanas

100g/3½oz/heaped ¾ cup raisins

120g/4¼oz/⅔ cup potato flour

100g/3½oz/heaped ½ cup rice flour

150g/5½oz/heaped ¾ cup chestnut flour

½ tsp sea salt, crushed

2 tbsp fruit sugar or caster sugar

1 tsp gluten-free baking powder

1 tsp xanthan gum

1 tbsp dried active yeast

50g/1¾oz dairy-free margarine, cut into cubes,
    plus extra for greasing

1   Put the sultanas, raisins and 250ml/9fl oz/1 cup water in a saucepan. Bring to the boil over a high heat, then turn the heat down to medium and simmer for 15–20 minutes until the fruit has softened and the water has been absorbed.

2   Sift the flours, salt, sugar, gluten-free baking powder, xanthan gum and yeast into a food processor with the dough blade attached and blend to mix together. Add the dairy-free margarine and blend again, then add 400ml/14fl oz/scant 1⅔ cups warm water and process for 10 minutes to aerate the dough. Add the softened sultanas and raisins and mix well. Transfer the dough to a bowl, cover with cling film and leave to rise for 30 minutes.

3   Preheat the oven to 200°C/400°F/gas 6 and lightly grease a 450g/1lb loaf tin with dairy-free margarine. Spoon the mixture into the tin and level the surface with the back of a spoon.

4   Bake for 20 minutes, then brush some water over the top with a pastry brush and cover with baking parchment, tucking the ends under the tin securely. Bake for another 20 minutes, brush again with water and then re-cover. Bake for another 5–10 minutes until cooked through. Turn the cake out of the tin and transfer to a wire rack and leave to cool for at least 10 minutes before serving.

baked treats

Packed with beta-carotene, butternut squash gives these scones moistness and texture. These are delicious with jam, fruit spread or even a savoury spread.

Butternut Squash Scones

Makes **6**   Preparation time **25 minutes**   Cooking time **40 minutes**

100g/3½oz butternut squash, peeled, deseeded
and cut into chunks

50g/1¾oz dairy-free margarine, plus extra for
greasing and to serve

85g/3oz/scant ½ cup rice flour, plus extra for
dusting

35g/1¼oz/¼ cup maize flour

35g/1¼oz/⅓ cup gram flour

½ tsp xanthan gum

2 tsp gluten-free baking powder

a pinch of salt

2 tbsp fruit sugar or caster sugar

1 tbsp unsweetened soya milk

jam, fruit spread or savoury spread, to serve

1 Put the squash in a steamer and steam over a medium-high heat for 15 minutes until soft.

2 Preheat the oven to 180°C/350°F/gas 4 and grease a baking sheet with dairy-free margarine. Sift the flours, xanthan gum, gluten-free baking powder, salt and sugar into a food processor with the dough blade attached and blend for 1 minute to mix well. Add the dairy-free margarine and blend for 2 minutes to mix, then add the soya milk and 75g/2½oz of the cooked squash and blend for 10 minutes. It will be very sticky.

3 Dust a chopping board liberally with rice flour. Scoop the dough onto the board and lightly roll it in the rice flour until workable. With the palm of your hand, press the dough out evenly to about 2cm/¾in thick. Using a 6cm/2½in round pastry cutter, cut out the scones, reworking the dough as needed.

4 Put the scones on the baking sheet and bake for 20–25 minutes until golden brown. Serve warm with dairy-free margarine and jam, or turn out onto a wire rack to cool before serving.

baked treats

Dinners

By the time we have put my daughter, Zoë, to bed in the evening,
it's generally getting late. So I want recipes I can put together with
minimal effort – whether it's for a meal by myself or with lots of people.
Here you'll find Herb- and Olive-Crusted Lamb, for example, that you
can whip up in no time at all; or recipes you can prepare ahead and keep
in the fridge or freezer until needed, like the Vegetable Tagine, the paste
for the Prawn & Butternut Squash Curry or the batches of sauce for the
Lasagne. And you'll also find some show-stoppers that look far more
difficult to make than they actually are, such as the Roasted Onion,
Fig and Lemon Thyme Tart or Duck with Plums.

Salmon en Croûte, page 138 >

This is wonderful for a weekend dinner, or even a Sunday lunch – and you can also use the stuffing with turkey for a gluten- and dairy-free Christmas meal.

Apricot- and Thyme-Stuffed Chicken

Serves **4**   Preparation time **30 minutes, plus making the stock**   Cooking time **2 hours 5 minutes**

125g/4½oz/⅔ cup unsulphured dried apricots, chopped

½ onion, chopped

1 garlic clove, crushed

200g/7oz/scant 1½ cups rice flakes

50g/1¾oz dairy-free margarine, diced, plus extra for greasing

1 tsp chopped thyme leaves, plus thyme sprigs to serve

1.8kg/4lb whole chicken

1 tbsp olive oil

250ml/9fl oz/1 cup Chicken Stock (see page 20) or stock made from gluten- and dairy-free stock powder

250ml/9fl oz/1 cup dry white wine

1 tbsp cornflour

sea salt and freshly ground black pepper

1   Put the dried apricots and 300ml/10½fl oz/scant 1¼ cups water in a saucepan and bring to the boil over a high heat. Turn the heat down to medium and simmer for 15–20 minutes, until the fruit has softened and the water has been absorbed. Transfer to a bowl and mix in the onion, garlic, rice flakes, dairy-free margarine and thyme. Season with salt and pepper.

2   Preheat the oven to 180°C/350°F/gas 4. Stuff the chicken and thread a cocktail stick or small skewer through the skin to secure, then put it in a large baking dish. Rub the oil over the chicken, season lightly with salt and pepper and add the stock and wine. Cover with baking parchment, making sure the ends of the paper are tucked under the dish. Bake for 1 hour, then remove from the oven and set aside the baking parchment.

3   Grease a small baking dish with dairy-free margarine, put any remaining stuffing in it and cover with baking parchment. Put the chicken and stuffing in the oven and bake for another 40 minutes until the juices run clear when the thickest part of the thigh is pierced with a skewer. If the juices look at all pink, bake for a little longer. Remove both dishes from the oven and cover the chicken again with the baking parchment, tucking the ends of the paper under the dish. Leave to stand at room temperature for 10–15 minutes.

4   Meanwhile, pour the pan juices into a small saucepan and bring to the boil over a high heat. Put the cornflour and 1 tablespoon water in a small bowl and stir until smooth, then stir it into the pan juices. Simmer, stirring occasionally, for 2–3 minutes until thickened. Season with salt and pepper. Serve the chicken and stuffing with the gravy and thyme sprigs.

dinners

Hearty, warming and wholesome – there's nothing like a great pie. Here I've used tarragon to add a subtle hint of aniseed to the chicken and leeks.

Chicken and Tarragon Pie

Serves **4**   Preparation time **15 minutes, plus making the chicken, sauce and pastry**
Cooking time **55 minutes**

2 tbsp olive oil

1 onion, chopped

1 leek, chopped

1.8kg/4lb unstuffed roast chicken
   (see page 106), cut into bite-sized pieces
   and juices reserved

1 handful of tarragon leaves, chopped

1 recipe quantity White Sauce (see page 12),
   substituting the juices from the chicken
   for some of the stock

brown rice flour, for dusting

1 recipe quantity Shortcrust Pastry
   (see page 19)

sea salt and freshly ground black pepper

1 Preheat the oven to 200°C/400°F/gas 6. Heat the oil in a large, heavy-based saucepan over a medium heat. Add the onion and cook, stirring occasionally, for 2–3 minutes until just starting to turn golden, then add the leek and cook for another 3–4 minutes until soft.

2 Transfer to a 2l/70fl oz/8-cup ovenproof casserole and stir in the chicken and tarragon. Heat the white sauce and stir it into the mixture, then season lightly with salt and pepper.

3 Liberally dust a chopping board with rice flour and roll out the pastry into a circle about 3mm/⅛in thick, and 3cm/1¼in wider than the casserole. Be careful as the pastry will still be slightly sticky. Ease the pastry onto the top of the casserole and cover the filling. If the dough seems too fragile to lift, simply turn the chopping board over to drop the pastry onto the casserole. Press the edges of the dough down gently to crimp and neaten the edge, using a sharp knife. Cut a small cross in the centre to let the steam out.

4 Bake for 40–45 minutes until the pastry is a rich, golden brown, then serve sprinkled with black pepper, if you like.

dinners

I love cashew nut cream! Here it gives thickness and creaminess to the curry and reduces the full-on heat of the spices and chillies.

Chicken Tikka Masala

Serves **4**   Preparation time **15 minutes, plus making the nut cream**   Cooking time **30 minutes**

2 tbsp olive oil

4 boneless, skinless chicken breasts, cut into
    bite-sized pieces

125ml/4fl oz/½ cup passata

½ recipe quantity Cashew Nut Cream
    (see page 13)

1 handful of coriander leaves, chopped

cashew nuts, chopped, to serve

½ red chili, deseeded and finely chopped,
    to serve

MASALA PASTE:

2 red chillies, deseeded

3 garlic cloves

2.5cm/1in piece of root ginger, peeled

1 onion, quartered

juice of ½ lemon

1 tsp ground cumin

1 tsp ground coriander

1 tsp turmeric

2 tsp garam masala

½ tsp chilli powder

1 tsp clear honey

50g/1¾oz dairy-free margarine

1 small handful of coriander leaves and stalks,
    coarsely chopped

1 tbsp tomato purée

2 tbsp olive oil

1   Put all of the ingredients for the masala paste in a blender or food processor and blend until a smooth paste forms.

2   Heat the oil in a large, heavy-based saucepan over a medium heat. Add the chicken and cook, stirring occasionally, for 5–6 minutes until lightly browned. Stir in the masala paste and passata, then turn the heat up to medium-high. When the mixture starts to bubble, reduce the heat to medium-low and simmer, covered, stirring occasionally, for 15–20 minutes until the chicken is cooked through.

3   Stir in the cashew nut cream and simmer, stirring frequently, for 3–4 minutes until heated through. Add a little water if the mixture becomes too dry. Sprinkle with the coriander leaves, cashew nuts and extra chilli and serve.

dinners

Umeboshi paste is made from pickled ume fruit, a type of Japanese plum. They have been called the kings of alkaline foods and help your body to digest foods properly and absorb nutrients fully.

Duck with Plums

Serves **4**   Preparation time **10 minutes, plus at least 2 hours marinating**
Cooking time **2 hours 50 minutes**

4 duck legs

8 shallots

16 plums, halved and pitted

3 red, orange or yellow peppers, deseeded and
    quartered

sea salt and freshly ground black pepper

MARINADE:

2 tbsp olive oil

4 tbsp tamari soy sauce

1 tbsp umeboshi paste

4 tbsp clear honey

3 star anise

1 cinnamon stick

1   Put the duck legs, meat-side down, in a casserole dish just large enough to fit them. Whisk together all of the ingredients for the marinade and pour it over the duck. Cover with a lid and leave to marinate in the fridge for at least 2 hours, preferably overnight.

2   Preheat the oven to 160°C/315°F/gas 2–3. Remove the duck from the fridge and, lifting the legs up as needed, put the shallots, plums and peppers on the bottom of the dish. Turn the duck legs meat-side up and season lightly with salt and pepper. Bake, covered, for 2 hours and 15 minutes until the meat is tender.

3   Remove from the oven and transfer the duck legs to a plate. Pour most of the juices from the casserole into a saucepan, discarding the cinnamon and star anise, and bring to the boil over a high heat. Turn the heat down to medium-high and simmer for 15–20 minutes until it has reduced by about half. Meanwhile, put the duck back in the casserole and bake, uncovered, for another 15 minutes. Remove from the oven and serve with the sauce.

dinners

This gluten-free version of the traditional slow-cooked recipe uses chorizo and pancetta instead of sausages, giving it an extra depth and richness.

Pork and Duck Cassoulet

Serves **4**   Preparation time **10 minutes, plus 12 hours soaking (optional) and making the stock**
Cooking time **4 hours 45 minutes**

200g/7oz/1 cup dried haricot beans or
    300g/10½oz/1½ cups drained tinned
    haricot beans, rinsed

2 duck legs

1 tbsp olive oil

150g/5½oz pancetta

450g/1lb pork fillet, cut into large cubes

2 tbsp goose fat

1 onion, finely sliced

4 garlic cloves, crushed

1 carrot, diced

2 bay leaves

1 heaped tbsp thyme leaves

1 heaped tbsp chopped rosemary leaves

2 handfuls of flat-leaf parsley leaves, chopped

650ml/22½fl oz/2⅔ cups Vegetable Stock
    (see page 21) or vegetable stock made from
    gluten- and dairy-free stock powder

225g/8oz chorizo, skinned and sliced

1   If using dried haricot beans, put them in a bowl, cover with cold water and soak overnight or for at least 12 hours, then drain and rinse well. Transfer to a large saucepan, cover with fresh water and bring to the boil over a high heat. Boil rapidly for 10 minutes, then turn the heat down to medium-low, cover with a lid and simmer for 1 hour until tender. Drain well.

2   Preheat the oven to 200°C/400°F/gas 6. Put the duck legs in a small roasting tin and bake for 30 minutes. Remove from the oven and turn the oven down to 140°C/275°F/gas 1.

3   Heat the oil in a large, heavy-based saucepan over a medium heat. Add the pancetta and fry, stirring occasionally, for 3–4 minutes until crisp, then remove, using a slotted spoon, and set aside. Add the pork to the pan and cook, turning occasionally, for 5 minutes until brown. Remove, using a slotted spoon, and set aside with the pancetta.

4   Melt the goose fat in the pan and then add the onion. Cook, stirring occasionally, for 2–3 minutes until just starting to turn golden. Stir in the garlic and cook for about 30 seconds, then add the carrot and herbs and cook for another 2 minutes. Add the stock and bring to the boil over a high heat, then lower the heat to medium and simmer for 2 minutes.

5   Put the duck in an ovenproof casserole, removing the skin first. Add the pancetta, pork, chorizo and beans. Add the stock mixture, stir well and bake, uncovered, for 3 hours. Remove the bones after 2 hours, stir and bake for another 1 hour. Remove the bay leaves and serve.

Soya cream has a fairly distinctive taste, but here the flavours of the pork, apple, lemon and white wine combine with it to create a delicious dish.

Pork in a Creamy Apple Sauce

Serves **4**   Preparation time **15 minutes**   Cooking time **20 minutes**

50g/1¾oz dairy-free margarine

750g/1lb 10oz pork fillet, trimmed of fat and cut
    into bite-sized chunks

3 apples

juice of ½ lemon

1 onion, finely chopped

1 garlic clove, crushed

100ml/3½fl oz/scant ½ cup white wine

125ml/4fl oz/½ cup soya cream

sea salt and freshly ground black pepper

1   Heat the dairy-free margarine in a large, heavy-based saucepan over a medium heat. Add the pork and cook, stirring frequently, for 5–6 minutes until well browned on all sides. Remove from the pan, using a slotted spoon, and set aside.

2   Peel the apples, cut into quarters and remove the cores. Slice each quarter into 3 slices and dip into the lemon juice.

3   Put the onion in the saucepan and fry over a low heat, stirring occasionally, for 2 minutes until just starting to turn golden. Stir in the garlic, then add the apple slices and cook for another 2–3 minutes, stirring occasionally, until golden. Return the pork to the pan and add the wine. Bring to the boil over a high heat, then reduce the heat to medium and simmer for 5 minutes. Stir in the soya cream, season lightly with salt and pepper and cook for another 2–3 minutes. Serve hot.

Amaranth is a fantastic gluten-free alternative to couscous. High in iron, calcium and protein, it also contains important phytonutrients that boost your immune system.

Lamb Burgers with Pomegranate Amaranth

Serves **4** Preparation time **20 minutes** Cooking time **40 minutes**

300g/10½oz/scant 1¼ cups amaranth

2 pomegranates

800g/1lb 12oz lamb mince

1 red onion, finely chopped

2 garlic cloves, crushed

½ tsp crushed chilli flakes

1 tbsp pomegranate molasses

2 large handfuls of flat-leaf parsley leaves, chopped

5 tbsp olive oil

100g/3½oz/⅔ cup pistachios, coarsely chopped

1 handful of mint leaves, chopped

juice of 2 lemons

sea salt

1 Put the amaranth and 750ml/26fl oz/3 cups cold water in a saucepan and bring to the boil over a high heat. Turn the heat down to medium and simmer, covered, for 15–20 minutes until the amaranth is tender and the water has been absorbed. Add a little more water if needed during cooking. Set aside.

2 Halve the pomegranates and set 3 of the halves aside. Hold the remaining half over a large bowl, bash the outer skin with a wooden spoon until all of the seeds fall out into the bowl. You'll need to bash the skin a few times before the seeds start to fall out, but they will. Put the lamb mince, onion, garlic, chilli flakes, pomegranate molasses and a small handful of the parsley in the bowl. Season with salt and mix well. Using your hands, divide the mixture into 8 equal pieces and shape each one into a burger.

3 Heat 1 tablespoon of the oil in a large, heavy-based frying pan over a medium heat. Add half of the burgers and cook for about 5 minutes on each side or until they are cooked to your liking. Remove from the pan, set aside and repeat with the remaining burgers and another 1 tablespoon of the oil.

4 Bash the outer skins of the remaining halves of the pomegranates over another large bowl. Add the pistachios, mint leaves, lemon juice, amaranth and remaining oil to the bowl and mix well. Serve with the burgers.

I've used anchovies for flavour in this recipe but they're also a great source of vitamins and minerals – and, more importantly, of omega-3.

Herb- and Olive-Crusted Lamb

Serves **4**   Preparation time **25 minutes**   Cooking time **30 minutes**

30g/1oz/scant ¼ cup capers in salt or brine

2 French-trimmed racks of lamb, each with
   8 cutlets

3 tbsp olive oil

30g/1oz drained anchovies in oil

100g/3½oz/heaped ½ cup drained black olives
   in brine

2 garlic cloves

1 tbsp tomato purée

1 handful of parsley leaves, coarsely chopped

1 small handful of basil leaves

heaped 2 tbsp amaranth

1   Preheat the oven to 200°C/400°F/gas 6. Rinse the capers and soak them in a bowl of water for 10 minutes, then rinse and drain well. If using capers in brine, just rinse and drain them.

2   Meanwhile, score the layer of fat on each rack of lamb. Heat 1 tablespoon of the oil in a heavy-based frying pan over a medium-high heat. Add the lamb and sear for 2 minutes on each side until browned all over, then transfer to a roasting tin, fat-side up.

3   Put the capers, anchovies, olives, garlic, tomato purée, parsley, basil and amaranth in a food processor and blend to form a finely chopped paste. With the motor running, add the remaining oil and blend until well combined. Spoon the mixture over the top of the fat, pressing down well with the back of the spoon.

4   Bake for 20–25 minutes, depending on how pink you like the meat. Remove from the oven and cover with baking parchment, ensuring the ends of the paper are tucked under the tin. Leave to stand for 5 minutes, then remove the baking parchment and serve.

dinners

Instead of a cooked herb crust, the steaks in this recipe are coated with fresh herbs. Their punchy flavours brighten up the dish and meld beautifully with the mushroom sauce.

Herb-Rolled Steak with Mushroom Sauce

Serves **4**   Preparation time **35 minutes**   Cooking time **20 minutes**

1 handful of mint leaves, finely chopped

1 handful of coriander leaves, finely chopped

1 large handful of flat-leaf parsley leaves, finely chopped

1 tbsp olive oil

4 fillet steaks

sea salt and freshly ground black pepper

MUSHROOM SAUCE:

25g/1oz mixed dried mushrooms, such as shiitake and porcini

15g/½oz dairy-free margarine

2 shallots, finely chopped

1 tbsp brandy

200ml/7fl oz/scant 1 cup dry white wine

60ml/2fl oz/¼ cup soya cream

1 To make the sauce, put the mushrooms and 300ml/10½fl oz/scant 1¼ cups cold water in a bowl and soak for 20 minutes. Strain through a sieve into a clean bowl and reserve the liquid.

2 Heat the dairy-free margarine in a heavy-based saucepan over a low heat. Add the shallots and fry, stirring occasionally, for 1–2 minutes until just starting to turn golden. Stir in the soaked mushrooms and cook for another 2 minutes, then add the brandy, followed by the wine and the reserved mushroom liquid. Bring to the boil over a high heat, then reduce the heat to medium and simmer for 15 minutes or until reduced by about half.

3 Meanwhile, mix the mint, coriander and parsley leaves together in a bowl and set aside. Heat the oil in a large, heavy-based frying pan over a medium heat. Season the steaks lightly with salt and pepper, add them to the pan and cook for 3–4 minutes on each side for medium-rare or 1–2 minutes longer for well done. Alternatively, brush the steaks with the remaining oil and cook under a hot grill.

4 Blend the sauce to a purée in a blender. Stir in the soya cream, season lightly with salt and pepper and cook for another 1 minute.

5 Roll the steaks in the herbs, covering them as much as possible. Serve immediately with the mushroom sauce.

dinners

Slow-cooking gives you the opportunity to use cheaper cuts of meat, yet still end up with wonderfully tender results.

Slow-Cooked Beef

Serves **4**   Preparation time **15 minutes, plus making the stock**   Cooking time **3 hours 40 minutes**

2 tbsp olive oil

800g/1lb 12oz casserole steak, cut into chunks

2 onions, finely chopped

2 large garlic cloves, crushed

750ml/26fl oz/3 cups dry red wine

250ml/9fl oz/1 cup Vegetable Stock
(see page 21) or vegetable stock made
from gluten- and dairy-free stock powder

25g/1oz dried porcini mushrooms

2 bay leaves

1 tbsp finely chopped rosemary leaves

1 tbsp finely chopped thyme leaves

2 tbsp kuzu

sea salt and freshly ground black pepper

1 Heat the oil in a large, heavy-based frying pan over a medium heat. Add the steak and cook, stirring occasionally, for 5 minutes until lightly browned. Remove the beef from the pan with a slotted spoon, transfer to an ovenproof casserole and set aside.

2 Preheat the oven to 150°C/300°F/gas 2. Add the onions to the pan and cook, stirring occasionally, for 2–3 minutes until starting to turn golden, then stir in the garlic. Add the red wine, stock, porcini mushrooms, bay leaves, rosemary and thyme and season lightly with salt. Cover and bring to the boil over a high heat. Pour the mixture into the casserole and stir. Transfer to the oven and bake, covered, for 3½ hours until the beef is tender.

3 Ladle most of the liquid from the casserole into a saucepan and heat over a medium heat. In a small bowl, mix the kuzu and 2 tablespoons cold water together to make a paste. Stir the mixture into the pan and simmer, stirring occasionally, for another 2–3 minutes until thickened. Season lightly with salt and pepper and remove the bay leaves. Stir the sauce into the beef and serve.

A gluten-free, dairy-free version of one of the all-time family favourites – my little angel, Zoë, adores this!

Lasagne

Serves **4**   Preparation time **10 minutes, plus making the sauces**   Cooking time **1 hour**

1 recipe quantity Roasted Tomato and Pepper
   Sauce (see page 12)
1 small handful of flat-leaf parsley leaves,
   chopped, plus extra to serve
500g/1lb 2oz minced steak

1½ recipe quantities White Sauce (see page 12)
300g/10½oz soya cheese, shredded
¼ tsp freshly grated nutmeg
12 no-pre-cook gluten-free lasagne sheets

1   Preheat the oven to 180°C/350°F/gas 4. Heat the roasted tomato and pepper sauce in a large
    heavy bottomed saucepan over a medium-low heat and add the parsley. Crumble in the
    minced steak and simmer for 8–10 minutes.

2   Put the white sauce in another saucepan, stir in the soya cheese and nutmeg and heat over a
    low heat.

3   Spread a third of the tomato sauce over the bottom of a 23 x 18cm/9 x 7in baking dish,
    then drizzle one-quarter of the cheese sauce over the top and cover with a layer of 6 lasagne
    sheets. Layer again with the tomato sauce, cheese sauce and 6 lasagne sheets. Cover with the
    remaining tomato sauce and the remaining cheese sauce, making sure that the cheese sauce
    covers everything on top.

4   Bake for 45–50 minutes, depending on the type of lasagne sheets used, until the cheese
    sauce is golden brown and the pasta is soft. Sprinkle with parsley and serve hot.

dinners

Fiery and fresh, this curry combines sweetness from the butternut squash and coconut and sourness from the kaffir lime leaves, lemongrass and lime.

Prawn and Butternut Squash Curry

Serves **4**   Preparation time **15 minutes**   Cooking time **30 minutes**

1 tbsp olive oil

250ml/9fl oz/1 cup coconut cream

400ml/14fl oz/scant 1⅔ cups coconut milk

1 tbsp tamari soy sauce

1–2 tbsp Thai fish sauce

500g/1lb 2oz butternut squash, peeled and cut into 2cm/¾in squares

500g/1lb 2oz cooked large king prawns

juice of 1 lime

1 small handful of coriander leaves, to serve

CURRY PASTE:

½ tsp cumin seeds

½ tsp coriander seeds

1 red chilli, coarsely chopped

2 shallots, coarsely chopped

2 garlic cloves, coarsely chopped

2.5cm/1in piece of root ginger, peeled and coarsely chopped

2 kaffir lime leaves

1 lemongrass stalk, coarsely chopped

½ tsp shrimp paste

zest of 1 lime

1 handful of coriander leaves and stalks, coarsely chopped, plus extra sprigs to serve

1   To make the curry paste, heat a heavy-based frying pan over a low heat. Add the cumin and coriander seeds and cook, stirring continuously, for 2–3 minutes until fragrant. Remove from the heat and grind to a fine powder with a mini food processor or spice mill. Add the chilli, shallots, garlic and ginger and blend well, then add all of the remaining ingredients for the paste and blend to form a coarse paste.

2   Heat a wok or large frying pan over a medium heat until hot. Add the oil and swirl it around, then turn the heat down to low and add the coconut cream and coconut milk. Cook over a low heat for 4–5 minutes. Add the curry paste and cook for 2–3 minutes, stirring well.

3   Add the tamari, 1 tablespoon of the fish sauce and the squash and cook over a medium heat for 12–15 minutes until the squash is tender. Take care not to let the mixture boil or the coconut milk will curdle. Stir in the prawns and cook for another 2–3 minutes until they are hot, then stir in the lime juice. Check the seasoning and add a little more fish sauce to taste if needed. Sprinkle with the chopped coriander and serve with extra coriander sprigs.

dinners

Not your standard risotto – this one combines the rich, sweet flavours of seafood with lemon zest and parsley to give it a herby, zingy freshness.

Seafood Risotto

Serves **4**   Preparation time **15 minutes, plus making the stock**   Cooking time **35 minutes**

800ml/28fl oz/scant 3¼ cups Vegetable Stock (see page 21) or vegetable stock made from gluten- and dairy-free stock powder

a pinch of saffron strands

4 tbsp olive oil

1 onion, finely chopped

2 garlic cloves, crushed

300ml/10½fl oz/scant 1¼ cups dry white wine

300g/10½oz boneless, skinless salmon, cut into bite-sized pieces

250g/9oz/1¼ cups arborio or other risotto rice

250g/9oz small scallops (or larger ones, cut in half horizontally), removed from their shells

250g/9oz raw, peeled king prawns

zest of 1 lemon

1 handful of parsley leaves, chopped

sea salt and freshly ground black pepper

1 Put the stock in a saucepan and bring to the boil over a medium heat. Remove from the heat, add the saffron and set aside.

2 Heat 2 tablespoons of the oil in a large, heavy-based saucepan over a medium heat. Add the onion and cook, stirring occasionally, for 2–3 minutes until just starting to turn golden. Stir in the garlic and cook for about 30 seconds, then stir in the wine and bring to the boil over a high heat. Lower the heat to medium, add the salmon and poach for 5 minutes or until cooked through. Remove the salmon, using a slotted spoon, and set aside.

3 Add the rice and 1 ladleful of the hot stock to the onion mixture. Cook over a medium-low heat, stirring continuously, until all of the liquid has been absorbed. Continue stirring in ladlefuls of the hot stock until nearly all of it has been absorbed. This will take about 18–20 minutes.

4 Meanwhile, put the remaining oil in a frying pan over a medium heat, Add the scallops and fry for 1–2 minutes on each side until golden brown or no longer translucent. Remove from the pan and transfer to a plate. Add the prawns to the pan and fry, turning occasionally, for 2–3 minutes until pink and cooked through. Remove from the pan and set aside with the scallops.

5 When the risotto is almost cooked, add the fish and seafood and season with salt and pepper. Stir in the lemon zest and cook for 2 minutes until the rice is soft but still has a slight bite, the fish and seafood are hot and all the liquid has been absorbed. Stir in the parsley and serve.

dinners

Cooking with banana leaves is a fantastic alternative to using aluminium foil, which contains heavy metals. They're available in many Asian speciality shops, but if you can't find any, you can use baking parchment instead.

Baked Sea Bass in Banana Leaf

Serves **4** Preparation time **15 minutes, plus 2 hours marinating** Cooking time **15 minutes**

2 tbsp olive oil

2 tbsp tamari soy sauce

juice of 1 lime

1 tbsp agave syrup

1 tsp shrimp paste

1 tsp freshly grated nutmeg

2 shallots, coarsely chopped

4 garlic cloves, coarsely chopped

3 lemongrass stalks, coarsely chopped

2.5cm/1in piece of root ginger, peeled and
    coarsely chopped

2 red chillies, deseeded and coarsely chopped

1 handful of mint leaves, plus extra to serve

1 handful of basil leaves

2 handfuls of coriander leaves and stems,
    plus extra leaves to serve

4 whole sea bass, cleaned

2 banana leaves, cut in half

1 Put all of the ingredients except the mint, basil, coriander, sea bass and banana leaves in a food processor. Blend to form a coarse, liquidy paste. Add the herbs and blend well.

2 Put a spoonful of the mixture in the cavity of each of the sea bass and put the fish in a non-metallic dish. Spoon the remaining mixture over the fish, cover and leave to marinate in the fridge for 2 hours.

3 Preheat the oven to 180°C/350°F/gas 4. Wash the banana leaves in cold water and lay one of them on a clean work surface. Put 1 of the sea bass on top, drizzle with a couple of spoonfuls of the marinade and wrap securely, fastening with string, if necessary. Repeat with the remaining banana leaves and fish and put them on a baking tray. Bake for 15 minutes, then serve.

dinners

Soya cream cheese is an excellent dairy-free ingredient that gives this dish smooth richness and great flavour.

Salmon Roulade

Serves **4–6**   Preparation time **20 minutes**   Cooking time **1 hour 5 minutes**

400g/14oz boneless, skinless salmon fillet

dairy-free margarine, for greasing

1 tbsp olive oil

2 shallots, finely chopped

1 recipe quantity White Sauce (see page 12),
    made with 500ml/17fl oz/2 cups
    unsweetened soya milk instead of stock

4 eggs, separated

zest of 1 lemon

juice of ½ lemon, plus extra wedges to serve

25g/1oz dill, chopped, plus extra to serve

50g/1¾oz soya cream cheese

400–500g/14oz–1lb 2oz smoked salmon slices

sea salt and freshly ground black pepper

1   Preheat the oven to 180°C/350°F/gas 4. Put the salmon in a casserole dish, cover with a lid and bake for 20–25 minutes until cooked through. Set aside to cool. Grease a 30 x 20cm/ 12 x 8in baking tray with dairy-free margarine and line the base with baking parchment.

2   Heat the oil in a large, heavy-based saucepan over a low heat. Add the shallots and cook, stirring occasionally, for 2–3 minutes until they start to turn golden. In another heavy-based saucepan, heat the white sauce over a medium heat, then remove from the heat and whisk in the egg yolks. Fold in the shallots and season lightly with salt and pepper.

3   Put the egg whites in a clean bowl and whisk until stiff peaks form. Add one-third of them to the egg-yolk mixture and whisk until well blended. With a metal spoon, carefully fold in the remaining egg whites. Pour the mixture into the baking tray and bake for 25 minutes until golden brown.

4   Meanwhile, put the cooked salmon, lemon zest and juice, dill and soya cream cheese in a food processor, season lightly with salt and pepper, bearing in mind that the smoked salmon will be salty, and blend well.

5   Remove the egg mixture from the oven and leave to cool for a few minutes. Remove it from the baking tray and remove the baking parchment. Turn it over and put it on a clean tea towel. Cover with a layer of smoked salmon, then spoon the cooked salmon mixture over the top and spread evenly. Using the tea towel to hold the base, carefully roll the long side of the roulade over until it forms a large sausage shape. Serve warm with lemon wedges and sprinkled with dill and black pepper, or leave it to cool, then wrap it in cling film and chill in the fridge for up to 12 hours before serving.

dinners

The combination of cornflour and polenta makes a lovely crisp, crunchy coating for the fish – and the rice flour gives the corn a delicate crunch.

Fish Goujons with Crispy Baby Corn

Serves **4**   Preparation time **15 minutes**   Cooking time **10 minutes**

85g/3oz/⅔ cup cornflour

2 large eggs

200g/7oz/1⅓ cups fast-cook polenta

1 tsp crushed chilli flakes

400g/14oz boneless, skinless white fish fillets,
   such as cod, sliced into strips

500ml/17fl oz/2 cups rapeseed oil

sea salt and freshly ground black pepper

CRISPY BABY CORN:

300g/10½oz baby corn

60ml/2fl oz/¼ cup soya milk

100g/3½oz/heaped ½ cup rice flour

250ml/9fl oz/1 cup rapeseed oil

1   For the crispy baby corn, put the corn in a steamer and steam, covered, over a high heat for 5–6 minutes until just tender but still crunchy, then set aside. Put the soya milk and rice flour in two separate bowls and season the rice flour with salt and pepper, then set aside.

2   Put the cornflour, eggs and polenta in three separate bowls. Lightly beat the eggs. Season the polenta with the chilli flakes and salt and pepper and mix well.

3   Dip each fish strip into the cornflour to coat well, then dip it in the eggs and then in the polenta. Transfer the goujons to a plate.

4   Dip each baby corn into the soya milk and then into the rice flour to coat well. Transfer to another plate.

5   Heat both quantities of oil in separate large saucepans or woks until very hot. To test if the oil is hot enough, drop 1 baby corn into the smaller quantity of oil. It should sizzle and begin to brown immediately. If not, remove it and leave the oil to heat some more. When the oil is hot enough, quickly put half of the fish goujons in the larger quantity of hot oil and half of the corn in the other, working in batches to avoid overcrowding the pans. Deep-fry the fish for 2 minutes or until golden brown and cooked through. Deep-fry the corn for 1½–2 minutes, turning half way through, until lightly golden. Remove the fish and corn from the oils, using a slotted spoon, and drain on kitchen paper. Serve immediately.

If you've struggled to find a recipe that works for cheaper, more sustainable types of fish, such as coley and pollack, this one might be the answer.

Fish Stew

Serves **4–6**   Preparation time **20 minutes, plus making the stock**   Cooking time **30 minutes**

2 tbsp olive oil

1 onion, finely chopped

4 garlic cloves, crushed

2 fennel bulbs, chopped

2 celery sticks, chopped

2 plum tomatoes, chopped

500g/1lb 2oz mussels

½ tsp cayenne pepper

a pinch of saffron strands

1 tbsp tomato purée

185ml/6fl oz/¾ cup dry white wine

375ml/13fl oz/1½ cups Fish Stock (see page 20) or stock made from gluten- and dairy-free stock powder, heated

1kg/2lb 4oz boneless, skinless white fish fillets, cut into large chunks

1 large handful of flat-leaf parsley leaves, chopped

sea salt and freshly ground black pepper

1 Heat the oil in a large, heavy-based saucepan or deep frying pan over a low heat. Add the onion and cook, stirring occasionally, for 2–3 minutes until starting to turn golden. Stir in the garlic and cook for 30 seconds, then add the fennel, celery and tomatoes. Turn the heat up to medium and cook, stirring occasionally, for 10 minutes or until the tomatoes have softened a little.

2 Meanwhile, thoroughly scrub the mussels under cold running water and rinse well. Remove the beards by pulling them towards the large part of the shell. If any of the mussels are open, tap them hard against a work surface and if they don't close, discard them.

3 Stir the cayenne pepper, saffron and tomato purée into the vegetables, then add the wine and stock. Season with salt and pepper, cover with a lid and bring to the boil over a medium-high heat. Turn the heat down to low and cook for 5 minutes until the fennel has softened.

4 Gently stir in the fish and cook for another 5 minutes, then add the mussels and press down gently so they are immersed as much as possible. Cover the pan and cook for 3 minutes, then remove and discard any mussels that haven't opened. Carefully stir in the parsley and serve.

This is a wonderful recipe for entertaining – you can make the pastry ahead of time and then simply whizz the herb paste together, spread on the salmon, and create a stunning dish effortlessly.

Salmon en Croûte

Serves **4**   Preparation time **15 minutes, plus making the pastry**   Cooking time **30 minutes**

50g/1¾oz dairy-free margarine, plus extra for greasing
1 large handful of rocket leaves
1 small handful of mint leaves
zest of 1 lemon

½ tsp sea salt, crushed
brown rice flour, for dusting
1 recipe quantity Shortcrust Pastry (see page 19)
500g/1lb 2oz skinned and boned salmon fillet
1 egg, beaten

1 Preheat the oven to 200°C/400°F/gas 6. Grease a baking tray with dairy-free margarine and cut a piece of baking parchment the same size as the tray. Put the dairy-free margarine, rocket and mint leaves, lemon zest and salt in a food processor and blend well.

2 Liberally dust a chopping board with rice flour and roll out the pastry into a large rectangle about 3mm/⅛in thick, and slightly more than twice the width of the salmon fillet. Be careful as the pastry will still be slightly sticky. Put the baking parchment over the pastry and hold it in place with one hand. Turn the board over and carefully put the baking parchment, with the pastry on top of it, on the work surface.

3 Put the salmon in the centre of the pastry and spread the herb mixture over it. Using a sharp knife, cut a 3–4cm/1¼–1½in square of pastry away from each corner of the pastry. Discard these pieces or use them to decorate the top of the pastry, if you like. Using the baking parchment to keep the pastry together, fold the two long sides of pastry over the salmon so that the edges overlap slightly. Carefully smooth the pastry along the seam with your fingers to secure it. Fold the two short ends of the pastry over just to seal the sides, trimming with a sharp knife if they are too long. Smooth the pastry at the seams again. Using a pastry brush, brush the egg over the top of the pastry, particularly at the seams and cut 3 slits in the top of the pastry. Transfer the parcel onto the baking tray.

4 Bake for 25–30 minutes until the pastry is golden brown, then serve.

Soya cheese is a brilliant dairy-free alternative. Here it provides protein and nutrients, but also a rich taste and a great texture for the covering layer.

Aubergine Parmigiana

Serves **4**   Preparation time **15 minutes, plus making the sauce**   Cooking time **1 hour**

4 aubergines, cut into thick rounds

2 tbsp olive oil

1½ recipe quantities Roasted Tomato and
  Pepper Sauce (see page 12)

1 small handful of thyme leaves

2 handfuls of basil leaves, chopped

200g/7oz soya cheese, grated

1   Preheat the oven to 180°C/350°F/gas 4. Put the aubergine slices on baking trays and drizzle with the olive oil. Bake for 30 minutes until golden brown.

2   Add the thyme and a small handful of the basil to the Roasted Tomato and Pepper Sauce and mix well.

3   Put a layer of the aubergine slices on the bottom of a baking dish and cover with one quarter of the tomato sauce. Sprinkle with a handful of the soya cheese followed by one quarter of the remaining basil. Repeat the layers three times ensuring that the soya cheese is sprinkled evenly each time, especially on the top.

4   Bake for 30 minutes or until golden brown on top, then serve.

dinners

Lemon thyme has an earthy, aromatic, citrus flavour that works well with the sweet taste of the roasted red onions in this tart.

Roasted Onion, Fig and Lemon Thyme Tart

Serves **4**   Preparation time **15 minutes, plus making the pastry**   Cooking time **1 hour 20 minutes**

dairy-free margarine, for greasing

2 red onions, each cut into 8 pieces

2 tbsp olive oil

brown rice flour, for dusting

1 recipe quantity Light Pastry (see page 18),
using sweet potato, instead of potato

4–5 figs, stems removed and quartered

80g/2¾oz firm tofu or soya cheese

2 large eggs, plus 5 large egg yolks

6 tbsp unsweetened soya milk

1 large handful of lemon thyme leaves, chopped

sea salt and freshly ground black pepper

1   Preheat the oven to 180°C/350°F/gas 4 and grease a 20cm/8in loose-based tart tin with dairy-free margarine. Arrange the onions on a baking tray and drizzle with the oil. Bake for 20–25 minutes until starting to brown.

2   Liberally dust a chopping board with rice flour and roll out the pastry into a circle slightly larger than the tart tin, to allow enough pastry for the side. Be careful as the pastry will still be slightly sticky. Neaten the edges with a knife, then ease the pastry into the tin, pressing down carefully to remove any air pockets. If the dough looks too fragile to lift into the tin, simply put the tin face-down on top of the pastry and turn the board over to drop the pastry into it. Neaten the edge again, prick the base all over with a fork, then line the pastry case with baking parchment and cover with baking beans. Bake for 8–10 minutes until just golden. Remove the pastry from the oven and remove the parchment and beans, then bake for another 2 minutes.

3   Spread the onions and figs over the pastry case, then crumble the tofu or soya cheese over the top. Whisk the eggs, egg yolks and soya milk together in a bowl, then mix in the lemon thyme and season lightly with salt and pepper. Pour the mixture over the onion, figs and tofu.

4   Bake for 30–35 minutes until the filling is cooked through. Remove from the oven and leave to cool in the tin for 5 minutes. Carefully ease the tart out onto a serving plate and serve.

dinners

A power-house of nutrients, packed with vitamins, minerals, protein and essential fatty acids, this recipe uses a gluten-free version of soba noodles, and miso paste and cornflour to thicken the sauce.

Buckwheat Soba Noodles with Tofu and Miso

Serves **4**   Preparation time **15 minutes**   Cooking time **25 minutes**

1 sheet of kombu

6 spring onions, white part only, finely sliced

2.5cm/1in piece of root ginger, peeled and
   finely chopped

2 tbsp tamari soy sauce

2 tbsp miso paste

300g/10½oz mixed exotic mushrooms, such as
   maitake and shiitake, sliced

2 pak choi, sliced widthways into thirds, stems
   and leaves separated

350g/12oz asparagus, woody ends discarded
   and stalks chopped

250g/9oz dried 100% buckwheat soba noodles

250g/9oz firm tofu, patted dry with kitchen
   paper and cut into bite-sized cubes

50g/1¾oz/heaped ⅓ cup cornflour

4 tbsp olive oil

1   Put the kombu, spring onions, ginger and 1l/35fl oz/4 cups water in a large heavy-bottomed saucepan. Cover with a lid and bring to the boil over a high heat, then reduce the heat to medium and simmer for 5 minutes.

2   Stir in the tamari and miso and then gently stir in the mushrooms, pak choi stems, asparagus and noodles, making sure the noodles are covered in the liquid. Cover and bring to the boil again over a high heat, then reduce the heat to medium and simmer for 8 minutes, stirring occasionally to make sure the noodles don't stick together. Add the pak choi leaves and cook for another 2–3 minutes until the noodles are cooked, the vegetables are tender and some broth is still left in the pan. Remove and discard the kombu.

3   Meanwhile, roll the tofu in the cornflour to coat evenly. Heat the oil in a large frying pan or wok over a medium high heat and add the tofu. Fry, turning occasionally, for 5–8 minutes until golden. Serve on top of the noodles, vegetables and broth.

Like all stews, the flavour of a tagine is enhanced when made in advance and then reheated. Store this in the fridge overnight or in the freezer for a couple of months for a wonderfully easy and convenient meal.

Vegetable Tagine

Serves **4**   Preparation time **15 minutes, plus at least 12 hours soaking (optional) and making the stock**   Cooking time **2 hours 15 minutes**

200g/7oz/scant 1 cup dried chickpeas or
    400g/14oz drained, tinned chickpeas, rinsed

2 tbsp olive oil

2 onions, finely chopped

2 garlic cloves, crushed

1 tsp cinnamon

1 tsp ground cumin

1 tsp ground coriander

1½ tbsp harissa

1 aubergine, chopped into large cubes

3 carrots, cut into batons

1 small butternut squash, peeled, chopped
    and deseeded

100g/3½oz/heaped ½ cup unsulphured dried
    apricots, chopped

250ml/9fl oz/1 cup Vegetable Stock (see page
    21) or vegetable stock made from gluten-
    and dairy-free stock powder

100g/3½oz/heaped 1 cup flaked almonds

1 handful of flat-leaf parsley leaves, chopped

sea salt and freshly ground black pepper

1 If using dried chickpeas, put them in a bowl, cover with cold water and soak overnight or for at least 12 hours, then drain and rinse well. Transfer to a large saucepan, cover with fresh water and bring to the boil over a high heat. Boil for 10 minutes, then turn the heat down to low and simmer gently, covered, for 1–1½ hours until tender. Drain well.

2 Heat the oil in a large, heavy-based saucepan over a medium heat. Add the onions and cook, stirring occasionally, for 2–3 minutes until just starting to turn golden, then add the garlic and cook, stirring, for another 30 seconds. Mix in the spices and harissa.

3 Add the aubergine and cook, stirring occasionally, for 5 minutes, then add the carrots and butternut squash and cook for another 5 minutes, still stirring. Add the apricots and stock, turn the heat down to low and simmer, covered, for 20 minutes or until the vegetables are tender, stirring occasionally.

4 Meanwhile, heat a heavy-based frying pan over a medium heat. Add the almonds and cook, stirring continuously, for 2–3 minutes until just beginning to brown.

5 Add the cooked chickpeas and parsley to the tagine and stir well. Sprinkle with the almonds and serve.

Butter beans are my favourite of all the beans. Packed with protein, fibre and low-GI carbohydrates, they have a firm texture and lovely, subtle taste that combines well with strong flavours.

Spanish-Style Butter Beans and Rice

Serves **4**   Preparation time **20 minutes, plus 12 hours soaking (optional) and making the stock**
Cooking time **2 hours 15 minutes**

300g/10½oz/1½ cups dried butter beans or 600g/1lb 5oz drained tinned butter beans, rinsed

6 tbsp olive oil

1 onion, finely chopped

2 garlic cloves, crushed

1½ tbsp smoked paprika, plus extra to serve

1 tbsp tomato purée

300g/10½oz/1½ cups brown basmati rice

350ml/12fl oz/scant 1½ cups dry white wine

600ml/21fl oz/scant 2½ cups hot Vegetable Stock (see page 21) or vegetable stock made from gluten- and dairy-free stock powder, plus extra if needed

6 tomatoes, halved

4 red peppers, quartered and deseeded

4 orange peppers, quartered and deseeded

100g/3½oz/heaped ½ cup pitted Spanish olives, chopped

1 large handful of flat-leaf parsley leaves, chopped

1   If using dried butter beans, put them in a bowl, cover with cold water and soak overnight or for at least 12 hours, then drain and rinse well. Transfer to a large saucepan, cover with fresh water and bring to the boil over a high heat. Boil for 10 minutes, then turn the heat down to low and simmer gently, covered, for 1–1½ hours until tender. Drain well.

2   Heat 2 tablespoons of the oil in a large, heavy-based saucepan over a medium heat. Add the onion and cook, stirring occasionally, for 2–3 minutes until just starting to turn golden. Stir in the garlic and cook for about 30 seconds, then stir in the paprika, tomato purée and rice.

3   Add the wine and stock to the pan, cover and bring to the boil over a high heat. Reduce the heat to medium and simmer for 35–40 minutes until the rice is soft but still has a slight bite and all the liquid has been absorbed. Add more stock during cooking, if necessary.

4   Meanwhile, preheat the oven to 180°C/350°F/gas 4. Put the tomatoes and peppers on baking trays and drizzle the remaining oil over them. Bake for 25 minutes until tender, then put the peppers in a bowl, cover with a plate and leave to stand for 5 minutes. Peel off the pepper skins and cut the flesh into chunks.

5   When the rice is almost cooked, stir in the peppers, tomatoes, butter beans and olives. When completely cooked, stir in the parsley. Sprinkle with paprika and serve.

dinners

Desserts

If you long to eat tarts or pies, cheesecake or creamy ice cream, look no further! Here you'll find mouth-watering dishes ranging from Passionfruit Curd Tartlets and Cherry Pie, to Blueberry and Lime Cheesecake and Chocolate Semifreddo. But while some of the desserts, like the Chocolate Fondant, are just pure indulgence, many of these recipes are healthy as well as delicious. Dive into Chocolate and Banana Soufflé, for example, instead of the classic chocolate version, Apple and Berry Crumble, or Summer Pudding, both packed with fruit, or Strawberry Pannacotta, made with nutrient-rich cashew nut cream. As my father used to say, it's a sad heart that never rejoices!

Blueberry and Lime Cheesecake, page 158 >

Gluten-free pastry tends to darken and burn very easily. This recipe needs longer in the oven than most tarts, so it's important to check on it towards the end of its time in the oven and cover it with baking parchment.

Pear and Almond Frangipane Tart

Serves **6–8**   Preparation time **20 minutes, plus making the pastry**   Cooking time **55 minutes**

75g/2½oz dairy-free margarine, plus extra for
   greasing
rice flour, for dusting
1 recipe quantity Sweet Shortcrust Pastry
   (see page 19)

50g/1¾oz/¼ cup fruit sugar or caster sugar
2 eggs
100g/3½oz/1 cup ground almonds
2 pears, peeled, quartered and cored
3 tbsp pear and apricot spread or apricot jam

1   Preheat the oven to 180°C/350°F/gas 4. Grease a loose-based 20cm/8in tart tin with dairy-free margarine and line the base with baking parchment. Liberally dust a chopping board with rice flour and roll out the pastry into a circle slightly larger than the tart tin, to allow enough pastry for the side, then neaten the edge, using a sharp knife. Be careful as the pastry will still be slightly sticky. Put the tin, face-down, on top of the pastry and turn the board over to drop the pastry into the tin. Ease the pastry into place, pressing down carefully to remove any air pockets, then prick the base all over with a fork. Line the pastry case with a piece of baking parchment and cover with baking beans.

2   Bake for 8 minutes until just starting to turn golden. Remove from the oven and remove the parchment and beans.

3   Meanwhile, make the filling. Put the dairy-free margarine and sugar in a large mixing bowl and beat, using an electric mixer, until light and fluffy. Gradually beat in the eggs, one at a time, then add the ground almonds and fold together with a spoon until well mixed.

4   Slice each pear quarter into 4 thin slices. Brush 2 tablespoons of the fruit spread over the base of the pastry case with a pastry brush, pour in the filling and cover with the pear slices. Cover the tin with baking parchment, making sure the ends are tucked under the tin.

5   Bake for 30 minutes, then remove the baking parchment. Gently brush the remaining tablespoon of the fruit spread onto the pears with a pastry brush and bake for another 10–15 minutes until the filling is set. Remove from the oven and leave to cool in the tin for 5 minutes, then carefully ease it out onto a plate and serve.

The soya cream works well with the spices, pumpkin and eggs, making a delightfully rich, creamy pie.

Pumpkin Pie

Serves **6–8**   Preparation time **25 minutes, plus making the pastry**   Cooking time **1 hour 30 minutes**

1.5kg/3lb 5oz pumpkin, sliced into 16 wedges, deseeded and fibres removed
dairy-free margarine, for greasing
rice flour, for dusting
1 recipe quantity Sweet Shortcrust Pastry (see page 19)

85g/3oz/½ cup fruit sugar or caster sugar
1 tsp cinnamon
½ tsp freshly ground nutmeg
50ml/1¾fl oz/scant ¼ cup soya cream
2 large eggs

1   Preheat the oven to 180°C/350°F/gas 4. Put the pumpkin on a baking sheet, skin-side down, and bake for 40 minutes or until cooked through. Remove from the oven and leave to cool for 5 minutes or until cool enough to handle, then scoop the flesh into a food processor and discard the skins.

2   Grease a loose-based 20cm/8in tart tin with dairy-free margarine and line the base with baking parchment. Liberally dust a chopping board with rice flour and roll out the pastry into a circle slightly larger than the tart tin, to allow enough pastry for the sides, and trim around the edges to neaten. Be careful as the pastry will still be slightly sticky. Put the tin, face-down, on top of the pastry, then, holding the board and tin together, turn them over to drop the pastry into the tin. Ease the pastry into place, pressing down carefully to remove any air pockets, then prick the base all over with a fork. Line the pastry case with a piece of baking parchment and cover with baking beans.

3   Bake for 8–10 minutes until just starting to turn golden. Remove the parchment and beans and bake for another 2 minutes. Remove from the oven.

4   Meanwhile, blend the pumpkin flesh for 5 minutes or until puréed. Add the sugar, cinnamon, nutmeg and soya cream and blend well, then add the eggs and blend until well mixed. Pour the filling into the pastry case. Bake for 10 minutes, then cover with a piece of baking parchment to help prevent the pastry from turning too brown. Bake for another 20–25 minutes until the filling is just set but still a little wobbly. Remove from the oven and leave to cool in the tin for 5 minutes, then ease it out onto a plate and serve.

I find that gluten-free pastry needs to contain more moisture than the normal kind, making it sticky and hard to handle. But if you use a chopping board and work quickly, you can even make a fully-encased pie like this one.

Cherry Pie

Serves 8–10   Preparation time **25 minutes, plus making the pastry and nut cream**
Cooking time **1 hour**

dairy-free margarine, for greasing

1kg/2lb 4oz cherries, stoned

100g/3½oz/heaped ½ cup fruit sugar
   or caster sugar

1 tbsp lemon juice

2 tbsp cornflour

rice flour, for rolling the pastry

1½ recipe quantities Sweet Shortcrust Pastry
   (see page 19)

1 egg or egg yolk, beaten

½ recipe quantity Cashew Nut Cream
   (see page 13) or soya cream (optional),
   to serve

1   Preheat the oven to 180°C/350°F/gas 4 and grease a 23cm/9in pie dish with dairy-free margarine. Put the cherries, fruit sugar and lemon juice in a heavy-bottomed saucepan and heat over a low heat, stirring occasionally, for 20–25 minutes until the cherries have softened. Put the cornflour and 2 tablespoons water in a small bowl and stir until smooth. Stir the cornflour mixture into the cherries and cook for 3–4 minutes until the juice thickens.

2   Liberally dust a chopping board with rice flour and set aside one-third of the pastry. Roll out the remaining two-thirds of the pastry into a circle slightly larger than the pie dish, to allow enough pastry for the sides, and trim around the edges to neaten. Be careful as the pastry will still be slightly sticky. Put the pie dish, face-down, on top of the pastry, then, holding the board and pie dish together, turn them over to drop the pastry into the dish. Ease the pastry into place, pressing down carefully to remove any air pockets. Neaten the edge, using a sharp knife, then pour the cherry filling into the pastry case.

3   Dust the chopping board again with rice flour and roll out the remaining pastry into a circle very slightly larger than the pie dish, to allow enough pastry to press down at the edges. Using a pastry brush, brush the rim of the pastry already in the pie dish with water. Using a spatula, ease the pastry onto the top of the pie and press down around the rim with your fingers to seal and crimp the edge. Brush the top with the beaten egg, then, using a sharp knife, cut a small cross in the centre of the top pastry to let the steam out during baking.

4   Bake for 30 minutes or until the pastry is a rich, golden brown. Leave to cool for 5 minutes, then serve hot, drizzled with cashew nut cream, if you like.

desserts

When I was growing up, I adored the lemon curd my mother used to make. This passionfruit version, inspired by her original recipe, has a wonderfully sharp, strong flavour for these tarts.

Passionfruit Curd Tarts

Serves **4**   Preparation time **15 minutes, plus making the pastry and 30 minutes cooling**
Cooking time **10 minutes**

100g/3½oz dairy-free margarine, plus extra for greasing
rice flour, for dusting
1 recipe quantity Sweet Shortcrust Pastry (see page 19)

80g/2¾oz/½ cup fruit sugar or caster sugar
1 large egg, plus 3 large egg yolks, beaten
6 passionfruits, halved
1 tbsp apricot jam

1   Preheat the oven to 200°C/400°F/gas 6 and grease four 10cm/4in tartlet tins with dairy-free margarine. Liberally dust a chopping board with rice flour and gently roll out the pastry to about 3mm/⅛in thick. Using a pastry cutter that is slightly larger in diameter than the tartlet tins to allow enough pastry for the sides, cut out 4 pastry circles, putting any extra pastry in the freezer for use another time. Be very gentle, as the pastry will still be slightly sticky. Lift the pastry circles into each tart tin (you may need to use a spatula) and press down gently to remove any air pockets. Neaten the edges, using a sharp knife, then line each pastry case with baking parchment and cover with baking beans. Put the tins on a baking tray and bake for 10 minutes or until firm and lightly golden.

2   Meanwhile, put the dairy-free margarine and sugar in a large heatproof bowl and rest it over a pan of gently simmering water, making sure that the bottom of the bowl does not touch the water. Heat, stirring occasionally, until the dairy-free margarine has melted, then scoop the passionfruit seeds into the mixture and add the eggs. Stir until the mixture thickens, then set aside to cool. (If you're not planning to serve the tarts straightaway, store the curd in the fridge once it has cooled.)

3   Remove the pastry cases from the oven and remove the parchment and beans. Leave to cool for about 3 minutes, then turn out onto a wire rack and leave to cool completely.

4   Spoon the curd into the tart cases and serve immediately. Keep any leftover tarts in the fridge for up to 1 day.

This wonderful cheesecake, filled with sweet blueberries and accented by zesty lime, rich soya cream cheese and spicy ginger biscuits, is a real treat.

Blueberry and Lime Cheesecake

Serves **4**   Preparation time **25 minutes, plus making the biscuits and at least 3 hours setting**
Cooking time **40 minutes**

100g/3½oz dairy-free margarine, melted, plus extra for greasing
1 recipe quantity Ginger Biscuits (see page 83), broken into pieces
300g/10½oz/2 cups blueberries

550g/1lb 4oz soya cream cheese
175g/6oz/1 cup fruit sugar or caster sugar
zest and juice of 2 limes
4 eggs

1   Preheat the oven to 180°C/350°F/gas 4. Lightly grease a deep 20cm/8in springform cake tin with dairy-free margarine and line the base with baking parchment. Heat the dairy-free margarine in a saucepan over a low heat until melted. Put the biscuits in a food processor and blend until the mixture resembles fine breadcrumbs. Add the crumbs to the melted margarine and mix well. Using the back of a spoon, press the mixture evenly into the base of the cake tin. Cover with the blueberries and leave to chill in the fridge for 10 minutes.

2   Meanwhile, blend the soya cream cheese, sugar, and lime zest and juice together in a food processor until smooth. Add the eggs and blend until smooth and creamy.

3   Pour the cheese mixture over the blueberries and bake for 30–35 minutes until pale golden brown and the top feels firm to the touch. Turn the oven off and leave the cheesecake to rest in the oven for another 30 minutes.

4   Ease the cheesecake out of the tin and leave to cool completely, then chill in the fridge for 3–4 hours until completely set before serving.

desserts

This is a great recipe for dinner with friends. Make the puddings the night before and use small, individual ramekins to create a stunning dessert.

Summer Pudding

Serves **4**   Preparation time **15 minutes, plus making the cake and at least 12 hours resting**
Cooking time **5 minutes**

750g/1lb 10oz summer fruit, such as
   raspberries, strawberries, blueberries
   and redcurrants

100g/3½oz/heaped ½ cup fruit sugar
   or caster sugar
1 recipe quantity Almond Cake (see page 95)

1   Put the fruit and sugar in a medium-sized saucepan and heat over a low heat, stirring occasionally, for 5–6 minutes until the fruit has softened and the sugar has dissolved completely. Take care not to overcook. Remove from the heat and strain, reserving the fruit in one bowl and the liquid in another.

2   Slice the cake vertically into thin slices with a long, sharp knife. Remove the crusts and cut 3 slices to fit the bases of four 175ml/5½fl oz/⅔-cup ramekins or pudding moulds. Press gently into the ramekins, so the cake covers the base. Press 3 or 4 more slices round the inside of each ramekin, pressing gently against the sides until covered completely.

3   Divide the strained fruit into the ramekins, filling them to the tops, then cover each one with a saucer and put a heavy weight on top. Chill the ramekins in the fridge overnight or for at least 12 hours. Reserve any leftover fruit to serve with the puddings.

4   Remove the weight and saucer from each ramekin and cover with an upside-down serving plate. Turn the ramekins over to turn the puddings out. Remove the ramekins and pour the reserved fruit liquid over the puddings, then serve immediately with any extra fruit, if you like.

160

This is melt-in-the-mouth delicious! When you take your first spoonful, you'll find a rich, gooey, chocolately centre inside.

Chocolate Fondant

Serves **4**   Preparation time **20 minutes**   Cooking time **20 minutes**

100g/3½oz dairy-free margarine, plus extra
    for greasing
200g/7oz dairy-free dark chocolate, 70% cocoa
    solids, chopped or broken into pieces
2 eggs, plus 2 egg yolks

100g/3½oz/heaped ½ cup fruit sugar
    or caster sugar
2 tbsp rice flour
heaped 2 tbsp gram flour

1   Preheat the oven to 180°C/350°F/gas 4 and grease four 175ml/5½fl oz/⅔-cup pudding moulds with dairy-free margarine. Put the chocolate in a heatproof bowl and rest it over a saucepan of gently simmering water, making sure that the bottom of the bowl does not touch the water. Heat, stirring occasionally, until the chocolate has melted. Remove from the heat, add the dairy-free margarine and stir until melted. Leave to cool for 10 minutes.
2   Meanwhile, beat the eggs and egg yolks together in a large bowl, using an electric mixer. Add the sugar and beat until thick and creamy. Using a large spoon, carefully fold in the melted chocolate mixture. Sift in the flours and fold until well mixed.
3   Divide the mixture into the pudding moulds and bake for 12–15 minutes or until risen and firm to the touch. Serve immediately.

desserts

Crumbles are so easy to whip up – and they make a wonderfully wholesome dessert all year round, whether you're using summer or winter fruit.

Apple and Berry Crumble

Serves **4**   Preparation time **15 minutes, plus making the custard**   Cooking time **40 minutes**

50g/1¾oz dairy-free margarine

4 apples, peeled, quartered, cored and cut into chunks

300g/10½oz/2 cups berries, such as blueberries or blackberries

3 tbsp clear honey

1 recipe quantity Custard (see page 13), to serve (optional)

CRUMBLE TOPPING:

150g/5½oz/heaped ¾ cup rice flour

2 tbsp maize flour

2 heaped tbsp gram flour

75g/2½oz/scant ½ cup fruit sugar or caster sugar

100g/3½oz chilled dairy-free margarine, cut into small cubes

1   Preheat the oven to 180°C/350°F/gas 4. Heat the dairy-free margarine in a large, heavy-based saucepan over a medium heat until melted. Add the apples and cook, stirring occasionally, for 10 minutes, then add the berries and honey. Cook, stirring occasionally, for another 5 minutes.

2   Meanwhile, make the crumble topping. Sift the flours into a food processor, add the sugar and blend to mix together. Add the dairy-free margarine and blend again until the mixture resembles fine breadcrumbs.

3   Spoon the fruit mixture into a baking dish and crumble the topping over, making sure all of the fruit is covered.

4   Bake for 20–25 minutes until browned on top. Remove from the oven and serve immediately with custard, if you like.

desserts

Here I've used xylitol to make the meringue because fruit sugar doesn't work. The xylitol creates a deliciously squidgy meringue, but if you'd prefer a crunchy, traditional one, simply use caster sugar.

Eton Mess

Serves **4**   Preparation time **30 minutes, plus making the nut cream**   Cooking time **1 hour 15 minutes**

800g/1lb 12oz/5⅓ cups strawberries, hulled

5 tbsp crème de cassis liqueur

35g/1¼oz/scant ¼ cup fruit sugar
or caster sugar

½ recipe quantity Cashew Nut Cream
(see page 13)

MERINGUE:

2 large egg whites

100g/3½oz/heaped ½ cup xylitol
or caster sugar

scant ½ tsp vanilla extract

1   Preheat the oven to 140°C/275°F/gas 1 and line two baking sheets with baking parchment. To make the meringues, beat the egg whites in a large clean bowl, using an electric mixer, until stiff peaks form. Gradually add the xylitol and continue beating until glossy, then beat in the vanilla extract.

2   Spoon the meringue mixture onto the baking sheets to make 6 meringues, spacing them well apart. Bake for 1 hour and 15 minutes until lightly golden brown, then remove from the oven and transfer the meringues to a wire rack to cool completely.

3   While the meringues are cooling, cut half of the strawberries into quarters and put them in a large bowl. Add 3 tablespoons of the crème de cassis, toss gently and leave to stand for 15 minutes.

4   Put the sugar and the remaining strawberries and crème de cassis in a blender and blend well. Strain the mixture through a sieve into a clean bowl to make a coulis.

5   Break the meringues into bite-sized pieces and put them in a large bowl. Gently stir the cashew nut cream into the quartered strawberries and liqueur, then fold the mixture into the meringues. Spoon into bowls or glasses, drizzle with the strawberry coulis and serve.

desserts

Don't be intimidated by soufflés – they are, in fact, easy to make as long as you whisk the eggs thoroughly and bake at the right temperature.

Chocolate and Banana Soufflé

Serves **4**   Preparation time **15 minutes**   Cooking time **20 minutes**

dairy-free margarine, for greasing

5 large egg whites

100g/3½oz/heaped ½ cup fruit sugar
   or caster sugar

100g/3½oz dairy-free dark chocolate,
   70% cocoa solids, broken into small pieces

1 tbsp cornflour

2 bananas

1   Preheat the oven to 180°C/350°F/gas 4 and grease a 2l/70fl oz/8-cup soufflé dish with dairy-free margarine. In a clean bowl, beat the egg whites, using an electric mixer, until stiff peaks form. Gradually add the sugar and continue whisking until glossy.

2   Put the chocolate in a large heatproof bowl and rest it over a pan of gently simmering water, making sure that the bottom of the bowl does not touch the water. Heat, stirring occasionally, until the chocolate has melted.

3   Put the cornflour and 1 tablespoon water in a small bowl and stir until smooth, then whisk it into the chocolate, using an electric mixer, until well blended. Mash the bananas, add them to the chocolate and mix well.

4   Using the electric mixer, whisk one-third of the egg whites into the chocolate mixture until well blended. Then, using a metal spoon, carefully fold in the remaining egg whites and mix well.

5   Pour the mixture into the soufflé dish and bake for 15 minutes or until very lightly browned on top and well risen. Remove from the oven and serve immediately.

desserts

Pistachios have a lovely texture and, along with the vanilla, they add specks of colour and sweet flavour to this dairy-free custard.

Pistachio Custard Bake with Roasted Figs

Serves **4**   Preparation time **15 minutes, plus making the nut cream**   Cooking time **40 minutes**

1 recipe quantity Cashew Nut Cream
    (see page 13)
2 vanilla pods, split and seeds scraped out, or
    2 tsp vanilla extract
12 figs or 4 large peaches
3 tbsp clear honey

4 large egg yolks
100g/3½oz/heaped ½ cup fruit sugar
    or caster sugar
175g/6oz/scant 1¼ cups pistachios, shelled
    and finely chopped

1   Preheat the oven to 160°C/315°F/gas 2–3. Put the cashew nut cream and vanilla pods and seeds, or vanilla extract, in a heavy-based saucepan and heat over a low heat for 5 minutes, stirring continually to make sure the mixture doesn't burn. Remove from the heat and discard the vanilla pods.

2   Put the figs in a baking dish and drizzle the honey over them. Bake for 25–35 minutes until soft, then remove from the oven and set aside.

3   Using an electric mixer, beat together the egg yolks and the sugar in a large mixing bowl until thick and pale. Beat in most of the pistachios, reserving a few to use as decoration. Add the nut cream mixture and 170ml/5½fl oz/⅔ cup water and beat until well mixed.

4   Divide the mixture into four 250ml/9fl oz/1-cup ramekins and put them in a large baking dish. Add enough boiling water to the dish to reach halfway up the sides of the ramekins. Bake for 30 minutes or, if using vanilla extract instead of vanilla pods, for 40 minutes until risen, firm to the touch and starting to turn golden.

5   Sprinkle with the remaining pistachios and serve immediately with the figs.

I've used cashew nut cream here for a thick creaminess and slightly nutty flavour – and agar agar flakes to set the pannacotta instead of gelatine.

Strawberry Pannacotta

Serves **4**   Preparation time **15 minutes, plus making the nut cream and 2 hours chilling**
Cooking time **10 minutes**

400g/14oz/2⅔ cups strawberries, hulled

1 tbsp agave syrup

**1 recipe quantity Cashew Nut Cream
(see page 13)**

**2 tbsp fruit sugar or caster sugar, plus extra as
needed**

1 vanilla pod, split and seeds scraped out

2 tsp agar agar flakes

1   Put the strawberries in a food processor or blender and blend for 2–3 minutes until smooth.
Strain the mixture through a sieve into a clean bowl to make a coulis and discard the pulp.
Put half of the coulis in a jug, add the agave and mix well. Chill in the fridge until ready to use.

2   Put the remaining strawberry coulis in a saucepan and add the cashew nut cream, sugar, and
vanilla pod and seeds. Heat over a low heat for 2 minutes, then taste and add a little more
sugar if needed. Sprinkle in the agar agar flakes and cook, stirring continuously, for another
5 minutes until the agar agar flakes have dissolved. Remove from the heat, discard the vanilla
pod and set aside to cool for about 30 minutes.

3   Line four 175ml/5½fl oz/⅔-cup ramekins with cling film. Spoon the cooled pannacotta
mixture into the ramekins and smooth the top with the back of a metal spoon. Cover with
cling film and leave to set in the fridge for at least 1½ hours. Turn out of the ramekins onto
plates and remove the cling film. Serve drizzled with the remaining coulis.

desserts

This is a deliciously subtle ice cream, with zesty lemongrass, kaffir lime leaves and lime juice combining with sweet mango. The key to this recipe is to use beautifully ripe mangoes.

Mango Ice Cream

Serves **4**   Preparation time **25 minutes, plus 8 hours freezing**   Cooking time **5 minutes**

500ml/17fl oz/2 cups soya cream

75g/2½oz/scant ½ cup fruit sugar or caster sugar

4 lemongrass stalks

25 fresh or dried kaffir lime leaves

1 tbsp cornflour

3 very ripe, large mangoes, plus extra sliced mango to serve

juice of 1 lime

1   Put the soya cream, sugar, lemongrass and lime leaves in a medium-sized saucepan and heat over a low heat until just starting to boil. Simmer for 2 minutes or until the sugar has dissolved, stirring frequently. Using a slotted spoon, remove the lemongrass and lime leaves and discard. Mix together the cornflour and 1 tablespoon water in a small bowl and stir until smooth. Add it to the soya cream and whisk for 2–3 minutes until the soya cream has thickened a little. Remove from the heat and leave to cool completely.

2   Using a sharp knife, carefully slice each mango down both sides, avoiding the stone. On the inside of each slice, cut the flesh into squares, cutting down to the peel but not piercing it, and scoop out with a spoon. Peel the remains of the mango and slice the flesh from the stone, setting some slices aside for serving. Put the remaining mango flesh in a blender or mini food processor and blend until smooth. Add the lime juice and mix well.

3   Using a large spoon, fold the soya cream mixture into the mango. Transfer the mixture to an ice cream maker and process according the manufacturer's instructions.

4   Alternatively, transfer the mixture to a large freezerproof container, cover with a lid and freeze for 2 hours. Whisk the mixture well, using an electric mixer, then return it to the freezer. Freeze for another 2 hours, then whisk again. Freeze for another 3–4 hours until completely frozen, or overnight.

5   Remove the ice cream from the freezer and leave to soften slightly for 10–15 minutes at room temperature, then serve with extra mango slices.

desserts

Whip up this wickedly rich and creamy frozen dessert and enjoy the natural feel-good properties of dark chocolate!

Chocolate Semifreddo

Serves 8–10   Preparation time **20 minutes, plus 30 minutes cooling and at least 3 hours freezing** Cooking time **15 minutes**

300g/10½oz dairy-free dark chocolate, 70% cocoa solids, chopped or broken into small pieces, plus extra chocolate shavings to decorate

100g/3½oz/scant ½ cup clear honey

2 tsp vanilla extract

500ml/17fl oz/2 cups soya cream

2 tbsp cornflour

1   Put the chocolate in a large heatproof bowl and rest it over a pan of gently simmering water, making sure that the bottom of the bowl does not touch the water. Heat, stirring occasionally, until the chocolate has melted. Stir in the honey and vanilla extract and mix well, then remove from the heat and leave to cool.

2   Meanwhile, put the soya cream in a medium-sized saucepan and heat over a low heat for 3–4 minutes until just starting to boil. Mix together the cornflour and 2 tablespoons water in a small bowl and stir until smooth, then add it to the soya cream and whisk for 2–3 minutes until the mixture has thickened a little. Remove from the heat and pour the mixture into the chocolate. Stir well, then leave to cool completely.

3   Line a 450g/1lb loaf tin with a large piece of cling film and pour in the semifreddo mixture. Cover with the cling film and freeze for 3–3½ hours or overnight until set.

4   Before serving, remove the semifreddo from the freezer and leave to soften slightly at room temperature for 10–15 minutes. Turn the semifreddo out onto a plate and remove the cling film. Slice and serve sprinkled with shavings of chocolate.

desserts

Index